Staying Strong

Diary of a Hurricane Maria Survivor in Puerto Rico

Sandra I. Roman

sandraroman3@gmail.com

ISBN: 1987480724
ISBN-13: 978-1987480726

Acknowledgments

I acknowledge my friend, editor and wonderful husband Michael. Your strength, patience, support and perseverance inspire me every day.

I acknowledge my daughters, whose lives fill mine with joy and desire to continue becoming a better version of myself.

I acknowledge my mom Aida, my brothers Alvin and Carlos, and my cousin, Maritza, who is like a sister. Thank you for always having my back when I need you.

I acknowledge my friend Yvonne Soong-Gunderson who was a rock for me to lean on during the hardest time of the Hurricane Maria survival period.

I dedicate this book to my dear country of Puerto Rico. May God give you the opportunity to be reborn into a better place for generations to come.

Table of Contents

Introduction

A friend once told me that any place you live will have its own risks of being hit by natural disasters. Some places have tornadoes, other places have forest fires, and there are areas prone to volcano eruptions and even earthquakes. At least hurricanes and tropical storms can be forecast, and we have time to prepare for them. This friend, like me, lives on this tropical island called Puerto Rico.

In Puerto Rico, the hurricane season runs from June to October, but most systems hit between August and September. In any given year, we worry about four or five storms, and maybe one becomes a hurricane that brings us a lot of rain and a day or two off from school.

So, when hurricane Irma hit on September 6, 2017, we were prepared. We put the storm shutters on our front windows, collected things from the yard and porch to prevent the wind from blowing them around, and looked for our flashlights and candles, just in case it got windy and our power got knocked out. On some islands like Barbuda, the devastation of Irma was like a bomb had gone off and destroyed most homes. In Puerto Rico, even though some areas were hit hard, most of us went about our business again within a day or two. By the end of that week, we were collecting donations to send to the towns in the Northeast of Puerto Rico, where Irma had caused the most damage.

Hurricane Irma went on to hit Florida with force while hurricane Jose moved about the Caribbean waters with a course not normally seen in Atlantic systems. After a few days, the media started giving us updates about hurricane Maria. It was rather unusual to have three active hurricanes at the same time.

We watched news of Maria the same way we have our entire lives. Not all systems follow the expected route. Some actually lose speed and intensity as they move, but not Maria. As time passed, the meteorologists grew more and more concerned. I remember watching Ada Monzón, a local meteorologist, on a Facebook video from a news channel. She was being recorded live from a hotel room as she looked at the latest bulletin from the National Weather Center. When she realized that Maria was a Category 4 hurricane and that it was going to pass over land, her voice trembled. She then reminded us that the last hurricane to hit Puerto Rico with similar force was Hurricane Georges in 1998. She urged people to take all the precautions needed to save their lives. At that point, I was glad my daughters were not watching that video with me; it would have been scary for them, I'm sure.

Chapter One - Remembering Hurricane Georges

Back in September of 1998, I was living in Des Plaines, Illinois. It was an exciting time in my life. I was engaged to be married to my future husband, Michael. After finishing a master's degree at Michigan State University, I was recruited immediately by a mining company called IMC Global in the northern suburbs of Chicago. I had landed my first job in my new field, Human Resources. I began working in their Bannockburn office, down the street from Michael Jordan's mansion, in June of that year.

After Georges, my family in Puerto Rico lost power. This was the norm after a big storm or hurricane. When it became evident that they would not have power for a while, I scouted local stores for a gas generator to ship to them, as the supply of generators on the island had been depleted. I managed to get a generator from a nearby Home Depot and went to the regional Fedex office to ship it home. I remember paying over $150 for shipping alone, even with some kind of employee discount program. It was probably the heaviest, most expensive piece of equipment I had ever mailed. My parents were on the receiving end; I would have shipped them heavy rocks if they had needed them. My parents had always worked hard and had made many sacrifices for my brothers and me, so I was eager to help them. By the time the generator arrived in Gurabo, Puerto Rico, my parents' home had power. So, the generator went to the home of my youngest brother, Carlos, who had a wife and five month old baby girl, all living in a small town without any power.

Carlos worked in the pharmaceutical industry, which often meant working rotating shifts and being away from his family at night. The Generac generator was a red and black work horse that was put to good use, as Carlos and his wife shared it with other neighbors to help them run their refrigerators. After Georges, their power was out for fifty-seven days.

Staying Strong

Back in 1998, I could not have imagined that, nineteen years later, my mother and my nephew would use that same generator for nearly three months after Maria to survive the darkness.

Chapter Two - Hurricane Maria

In this era of social media and cell phones, we can easily become dependent on our devices to communicate with our loved ones. Our island is no exception; Facebook, Twitter and Instagram have millions of users in Puerto Rico. Even though we live on a small island, traveling from one region to another requires a lot of time because of our geography. Also, there are too many vehicles per capita, which negatively impacts how often people travel outside of their immediate region.

Traveling fifteen miles can easily become a forty-five minute, bumper-to-bumper trip. This limits how often people visit their family members or friends who are not in their immediate vicinity. And when you think of all the Puertorricans living abroad, our fondness for social media is a bit more understandable. Our family is no exception; we keep in touch with dozens of friends, former co-workers, and relatives through social media.

When a natural disasters hits, the news always shows the worst-hit areas. Floods, destroyed buildings, upside down cars -- those are the images that make it to the papers and TV news reports. We know that tragedy, like violence, sells. Having lived in the U.S. during Hurricanes Hugo and Georges, I knew firsthand what happens when a hurricane hits the island and you cannot get in touch with your loved ones. Anxiety grows, and you start to worry about your family suffering in the distance. Every day that goes by without hearing from your family makes you imagine the worst possible scenarios. You can literally grow sick with worry.

Anticipating this, I posted the following message in my Facebook status the day before Hurricane Maria arrived.

Dear family and friends;

We are preparing for the imminent arrival of Hurricane Maria. Our first preparation was humbly bowing in prayer asking God to have mercy on us.

We have non-perishable food for several days and a water tank on the roof of our house that provides us clean, potable water whenever water service is unavailable.

We have lanterns and candles and plenty of board games and projects to keep us busy during the day-and-a-half that Maria is predicted to last.

Electric power is very likely to stop working as early as tonight. This means we won't have working internet, home phone, or electricity at our house.

If AT&T loses power or antennas, our cell phones may stop working altogether. We may be off the grid for a week or so. Please do not worry too much if we don't post here; it just means we have no connection.

Keep us in your prayers for God to protect us and that we may exhibit the fruit of the Spirit in the forms of patience and kindness to those around us.

We are standing firm on the rock who protects us, whose name is Christ.

Sandra

Thinking back upon those words, I had an idea of how the next 24-48 hours would be, but I could not even have imagined the extent of the devastation Maria would bring to our country or how long it would take us to recover from the damage.

September 19, 2017, was a Tuesday. The girls didn't go to school. Classes were cancelled in anticipation of the rain and traffic that would most likely start that afternoon. I told the girls that we should use our electronics and try to finish whatever work we were doing while we had power. I remember working on the program for an event at our church. I managed to finish the program in the computer, in case I had no power to print it later in the week. Little did I imagine that this particular event would be cancelled and not rescheduled for another seven months. We also finished doing our laundry, as both our washer and dryer are electric.

We moved furniture away from the walls, moved the dog water bowl inside, put away the hammock and the grill. I placed smaller items in the outside bathroom, so they would not be blown about by the winds.

Michael finished putting the storm shutters back up, as we had kept some of them up from Hurricane Irma. This time, he also protected the front door, as we knew Maria would bring stronger winds. Our front door is a mix of metal and glass. It's actually a double door, but we normally only use one side of it, and the other side remains closed.

According to the National Weather forecast and other tools that I checked online, the worst of Maria would pass over our town in the early afternoon hours of Wednesday.

I don't recall exactly at what time the rain started that Tuesday. It rained like it does frequently during hurricane season on our beloved island -- not too heavily at first. Some mild winds started blowing and, before night came, the power was out at our house in the Turabo Valley, which is about fifteen miles south of San Juan.

Irene and Lydia asked if they could sleep in our bedroom. We arranged their sleeping bags on the floor of our bedroom. We prayed together and went to bed early. As the night went on, the rain and wind persisted and the thunder and lightning began. Sugar, our dog, always goes crazy with anxiety when thundering begins. He was sleeping in the floor of our bedroom also, but would run in and out of the room to bark at the sound of thunder. I would wake up to his barking and then fall back to sleep.

Around four in the morning of Wednesday the 20th, my husband and I woke up. Sugar had been made very nervous by the sounds outside. The wind was howling loudly, and it sounded like an animal. I had never heard such sounds before. It sounded like something out of a horror movie. It was pitch black outside.

Something made out of metal was banging in our backyard. Michael was guessing that it would be the storm shutters that he didn't use. I was afraid to ask where he had left them, but he explained that he had left them on the roof of the house, held down with bricks. I was imagining those thin pieces of metal flying about the neighborhood. The rain and wind were hitting the metal windows of our room hard. Irene, our oldest, woke up with the commotion, but Lydia slept through it. There was nothing we could do, so we went back to bed.

Michael sleeps much lighter than I do. He must have heard the wind rattling the doors in the living room. When he got to the living room, he found what we later discovered was a familiar scene in many homes: the wind was threatening to blow the front doors open. The wind found a way to sneak through the bottom of the storm shutter, and our heavy metal and glass doors were bowing in. Michael's problem solving skills went into full gear and adrenaline kicked in, because he moved the living room cabinet back to make room for our heavy sofa, then pushed the cabinet back to wedge the sofa against the front door. I believe that it was also when he had the presence of mind to record the wind blowing past our glass dining room door. He was concerned that the doors might explode. Our home faces east. The rain and wind looked like curtains passing across the porch from front to back.

When the girls and I got up that morning, it was so cloudy that it looked like nighttime. Michael went into the bathroom and heard some gurgling noises from the roof, which made him realize he had better check our roof drains. At about the same time, Irene stepped into a puddle on the way to her room.

The rain water was accumulating on the roof of our house and water was leaking in at various places. I didn't want Michael to go up onto the roof during the hurricane, but we had no choice. He was careful and fast. He came down the metal extension ladder after having unclogged the drains that were full of debris. Thankfully, the metal noise in the back yard from the early hours had not come from our unused storm shutters, but rather part of our neighbors' roofing.

This must have been when the eye of the storm was passing near us. Even though it didn't stop raining completely, it was a break from the heavy rain.

Homes in our development were built in the 1980's and are made of concrete, but many houses have added porches or decks that were finished with zinc roofing. Later that day, we found that many such additions were blown to pieces all over the neighborhood.

We ate something cold for breakfast. It was so windy out on the porch that we didn't try turning on the gas grill to make coffee. We got our raingear on and ventured out to our side porch and the backyard. It looked like somebody had plowed through our backyard, taking down our avocado tree and most of our banana plants. There was only a puddle filled with lemons where our lemon tree used to be. We later found the tree in our neighbor's yard.

As the day went on, we tried to find out what was happening in the rest of the country. We didn't have a battery powered radio, so I got into my car and listened to the only radio station that was on air. It was very frustrating. I listened to it for half an hour, and there was no real news. They were sort of stating the obvious: that it was a large system and had affected the whole island. Police were asking people not to leave their homes, and they even started talking about what was later officially announced: a three day total curfew.

Michael is the kind of person who does not like to procrastinate, so as soon as it stopped raining, he started cleaning all the debris and fallen trees from the backyard. Around 4:00 p.m., I realized that my headache was probably related to lack of caffeine, so I made coffee the old-fashioned way on the gas grill. The poor old grill had survived being thrown about our porch by the wind. And good thing it did! At that point, I had no idea that I would have to cook three meals a day on the grill for the next three months.

Later that afternoon, I ran into our next-door neighbor, David, who had ventured out into the neighboring town of Gurabo. David's father-in-law, Don Aniel Lugo, runs a print shop across the street from my mother's home. David and his wife, Lillian, had gone over to check on the shop, and they had spoken to my mom. So, at that point, I knew that my mother and my brother were OK. This was the beginning of bringing back old customs from the 1940's, before phones were accessible to everyone, when people would send messages with friends and neighbors whenever they ran into each other.

I later found out that, during the morning of the hurricane, my mother and my nephew had heard noises coming from across the street. Don Aniel's print shop had a metal rolling door for the warehouse area, and the door had been forced open by the wind. My nephew, Alvin, Jr., went over to try to close it, but the wind had damaged the shape of the frame and the door would not roll down properly. When Mom called Don Aniel, he was about to call her, wondering about damage to his shop.

Don Aniel lives not too far from Mom, but his neighborhood was built around existing trees and creeks. A very pretty set up, but now it had become their prison. They could not drive out, because all the nice grown trees were now fallen and blocking the roads.

The warehouse does not have a security guard. Like many businesses in Puerto Rico, the watchful eye of a good neighbor is all the security needed.

AT&T's generators must have gone out, because, in the midst of the hard winds on the morning of the 20th, we had signal, enough to send text message and post online. However, later that day, the phones had no service, no signal, nothing. The dreaded "No Service" message appeared where the cell phone bars normally show up on our phones.

As the hours turned into days, with no other way of communicating, we defied the three-day curfew and visited my mother. It was chaotic trying to drive anywhere on the island. Concrete posts were down; power and phone lines were down. It was heart-breaking to see the devastation. Our once-green mountains were now brown, as if a forest fire had burned them. Store fronts were destroyed, homes were missing tin roofing, and there were brand-new cars with broken windshields in the dealerships with debris all over them. The roofs of many malls and big-box stores had given in due to the winds. Air-conditioning units were ripped off roofs, and water damage was the order of the day everywhere.

Chapter Three - Our New Normal

It wasn't raining anymore in our valley. The heat was unbearable, and the mosquitoes were out in force. There was nothing you could do but wait for things to normalize. There was nothing cold to drink, no fans to cool you off or blow the mosquitoes away.

The situation was dire, but more so for the poor, who rely on food stamps or live paycheck-to-paycheck. Food stamps are like debit cards: once a month, the federal government deposits funds in the accounts of the beneficiaries. With all systems down, those cards were useless.

Those first few days, there was no help for people in such situations. Neighbors and family members had to help each other out. Even with money in the bank and food in the supermarkets, many stores were closed, and the banks' automatic tellers were not working due to the lack of power across the island.

Other than cleaning, surviving, and trying to find news, there was not much to do during the first few days following Maria. I wrote the following message to update our friends via Facebook, but it took a couple of days before I could find cell signal to send it:

September 23, 2017

> *Dear friends and family,*
>
> *It's been four days since Hurricane Maria hit Puerto Rico with winds of over 150 miles per hour.*
>
> *It was a very long night and day. The slow-moving beast came pretty much right over our city, ripping up trees, electric lines, and tin roofs and causing entire forests to look brown instead of their usual green. The winds were roaring, and we could not but just wait until morning. Our front door nearly gave in, but quick thinking*

on Michael Richter's part saved the house from wind and rain.

We lost our grown trees and our fence and had some water damage from the rain that gathered on our roof when all the drains got full of leaves and flying debris.

We found antennas, dog cages, Christmas lights, and part of our neighbor's porch roof tangled in our yard.

But, all in all, we are doing fine. We have had no power since Tuesday, and our water comes from our water tank that we have on our roof. The water comes down via gravity. We think it's like 600 gallons in reserve.

Our church lost the roof of the kitchen and suffered other damage, but it did not flood. The worst of the damage I think was to the electric lines and air conditioners, besides the kitchen.

The girls' school seemed to have suffered some damage, but it stands.

So far, my brother, niece, nephew, mom, and aunt who lives nearby are all doing well.

All in all, we will be able to recover from this soon. There are hundreds of families that will not; their tin roofs flew away and all their belongings got water damaged.

The hardest systems hit were power and communications. Our phones have no signals since Wednesday the 20th.

Some people are powering their homes with generators, but we do not own one. Generators require gasoline or diesel to operate. Many gas stations are still closed.

Those that are open have lines that are miles long and often run out of gas within hours.

There are lines at grocery stores and markets. Without power, they struggle to provide service -- no lights, no refrigeration, and no ATM service. Sales are cash only.

The government established a three-day, all-day curfew, which they could not really enforce. Now it's been modified to just nighttime. They hope the National Guard and the Feds can help enforce it.

Our routines have changed a lot in just a few days. We get up at first light, prepare breakfast on the one burner of our gas grill, and set out to do our chores or errands during daylight hours.

An example of our errands was visiting our local bakery and standing in line for about 45 minutes for the maximum two loaves of bread. It was hot in the bakery, as their ovens were going but their AC was not. People waited patiently, hungry but happy to be alive.

Cleaning yards takes a good two days if you have a small one. Then there is visiting relatives, friends, and neighbors, because you cannot call them. And we have been giving away avocados, bananas and lemons from our fallen trees that were mid harvest.

After dinner, we rush to shower with daylight, using a bucket and a cup. Then we play board games and drink hot chocolate.

We finish our nights with Bible reading, singing and prayer, thanking God for his strength, hope, and joy in the midst of such devastation. We also pray for those who have lost their homes and the workers who are trying to restore roads and services. And for the relatives of the ten people who died during and after the hurricane.

Then we try to sleep the best we can with the heat and humidity on full power unless a night time rain shower comes by to give us a break.

We had to drive fifteen miles to San Juan in order to find cell service to share this news with you. Please pray for Puerto Rico. Pray that all the aid that is arriving is properly and justly distributed to those who need it the most.

If you are interested in donating to a family in need or towards our church building repairs, please let me know. Money is what is most needed. I can personally make sure that your donation goes 100% to fill the need that you wish to support.

It may still be a while until we get cell phone service, and it may be weeks until we get power back in our home. Please pray for patience, creativity, and for God to continue to provide and care for us.

We'll remain strong with God's help.

Hugs,

Sandra and family

Chapter Four - Off the Grid

I knew that our family in the States must have been pretty worried. My oldest brother Alvin had a working router in his home. His cable and internet provider had underground connections that were still working in some areas. Whenever his neighbor would turn on his gas generator, allowing Alvin to plug in a couple of appliances, he could get his phone to connect via Wi-Fi. That is how my brother Carlos, living in Oregon at the time, could get news from the family. I thought about driving to Alvin's house in order to connect and reach out to my husband's family, but then I realized that I would have to do so at night when his neighbor was home and had the generator running. It was too dangerous going out at night, and one can run the risk of getting arrested from breaking curfew.

Our golden opportunity came on day four after the hurricane when we were visiting my mother. We knew at that point that there was a particular phone company that had phone signal in some areas of the island. A young couple was walking past my mother's house, so she approached them and asked them if their phone was working. They said yes, so she asked if we could use it to make a phone call to our relatives in the states.

My mom always says that nothing is lost by asking; all that people can say is "No," and then you are no worse than you were before. So when they politely agreed, Mom handed me the phone. I had to think fast. Which of Michael's relatives was most likely to answer their cell phone on the first attempt? I knew then that Richard was my safe bet. Richard is a doctor and therefore he is used to having a cell phone nearby for emergencies and on-call situations. He was so happy to hear from us. The first thing he said was, "we were so worried about you guys." We kept the call short out of respect for the unknown couple that had agreed to lend us their phone. My brother-in-law agreed to call Michael's parents and sister to let them know we were fine.

One thing that we experienced immediately was a sense of brotherhood (and sisterhood) among neighbors and friends. We knew we were in it together, and the least we could do was share with our neighbors. Extension cords going from a house to the one next door or across the street was a common scene everywhere we visited. Power generators disappeared from the store shelves, and many stores were not even open. Puertorricans everywhere started sharing their generators and their gasoline. People cooked in their camping stoves and shared a plate of food with their neighbors.

Caring is embedded in our culture. Sometimes people are annoyed by how much people mind and interfere in their lives. However, in times of need there is nothing better than to belong to a community that cares.

Chapter Five - Let the Status Updates Begin

A couple of days after making contact with my bother-in-law, we were driving home from my mother's when I noticed some cars were pulled over on the highway's emergency lane. My next thought was, "They are stopped here because there must be signal for the phones." Sure enough, for the first time in five days our phones were more than just fancy flashlights -- there was signal. The signal was weak; it was easier to connect to the internet or send text than to maintain a phone conversation. It was also unstable and would disappear if you moved away from the reach of the few antennas that were working. The next update I shared on Facebook was the following message:

Monday Sept 25th

Today is the 5th day since Hurricane Maria. We are now living a much simpler life. A life where there is no running water, no power, no phone, and no cards are accepted at most businesses.

We are rationing the water from our cistern, since we have no idea when the water company will have electricity in order to run their pumps.

When we rinse our dishes or wash our hands, we collect that used water in a bucket to flush our toilets.

Today's main errand was to go grocery shopping. We had enough cash that we decided we could use some for food. Part of the challenge was to buy only things that require no refrigeration. Enough to feed four people three times a day, plus snacks for 4-5 days.

Drove to the closest grocery store with our list in hand, not knowing if we would be able to go in and shop ourselves or, like at some stores, if we would have to hand it in and wait for an employee to bring us the goods to the door.

Thank goodness, the store was opened. There have been delays with the distribution of diesel. Some businesses are closed, because without diesel they cannot run their generators.

The girls and I waited in line, outside the door. There were about 40-50 people waiting. The store had a porch type structure that provided shade, and it was cloudy and not too hot when we arrived at 10:00 a.m. As usual, I started talking with the person in front of me in line. I found out that he worked at the local Home Depot. He said the hurricane destroyed some structural parts of the stores when the AC units blew off and the winds went in, causing a tornado like effect inside the building.

The girls helped me find the items on our list, and, in about an hour, we were out the door with almost everything on the list, including one box of 24 bottles of drinking water. Water was the only item that was restricted.

Our menus for this week;

*Bacon sandwiches (fully cooked bacon does not need refrigeration).
*Coffee and hot chocolate with evaporated milk
*pasta with cooked chicken sausage
*pasta with canned chicken and Alfredo sauce
*canned vegetables
*potatoes and yams with salted cod fish prepared with oil, onions and avocado.
*rice with canned sausage and kidney beans
*peanut butter and jelly sandwiches

*crackers
*chips and guacamole (home made from the tree that Maria took down)
*canned soup
*cookies
*pop tarts
*water

Our stove is our BBQ grill and its one gas burner.

Our fridge is empty and clean. Ice is a commodity, of which we have none.

Keep praying, please, and more so for those who lost their homes or their jobs.

Staying strong,

Sandra

When we realized how bad the situation was and that it would last more than just a week or two, our next thoughts were to find things to occupy ourselves with in the long days to come. We looked for books, games, craft projects, and toys that require no electric power. Irene, our oldest, is an artist. Within a couple of days she had begun a pencil drawing and a water-color painting of the tree that was still standing in our neighbor's back yard.

Thankfully, we had enough gasoline and cash at hand that we didn't have to stand in a huge line immediately after the hurricane. We did eventually stood in line at the bank for an hour, in the sun, in order to get $300. That was the maximum allowed by the banks that were open.

While waiting in the bank line, people would talk about their experiences. Many of them came from towns an hour away, because the banks in their towns were not open and the ATMs closest to them were not working.

It broke my heart to see so many elderly people standing in lines for hours while the managers of stores and banks followed their ridiculous safety guidelines developed by folks who were comfortably seated in an air-conditioned board room somewhere with no clue of the hardship that we were experiencing.

Wednesday Sept 27th

Our phone signal is still unstable. Please do not worry if we lose touch. We are fine. Fighting the good fight and staying strong in the faith.

Chapter Six - Stress and Anxiety on High

By this point, I started noticing that our relatives in the U.S. were showing great concern for our wellbeing. Having been in their place during Hurricanes Hugo and Georges, I knew that they were watching the daily news in horror. The media was probably focusing on the humanitarian crisis that many were going through on the island. The inability to act in favor of your loved ones combined with the empathy that you feel when you see suffering on TV daily leaves people with an empty feeling of impotence and frustration.

I suspected these feelings were hitting my brother Carlos and my mother-in-law Pauline especially hard. My brother described his feelings when he went to work the day after the hurricane. At the Intel facility near Portland, Oregon, where he worked, not many people were even aware of what his home country was going through or that it even was hit by a hurricane. Carlos had moved to Oregon in 2016, but his whole family, including his two daughters, was on the island during the hurricane. With this in mind, I decided to continue posting detailed accounts of our reality, being careful not to add more reasons for them to worry or be sad. After all, this was not the first time in my life that I faced hardship. Just like in previous times, I relied on God, our rock and the source of our strength.

> *Thursday September 28th*
>
> *Entertainment during hard times:*
>
> *Our culture is filled with laughter, music and social interaction. Talking to strangers is more than normal here; it's expected.*
>
> *The aftermath of Hurricane Maria has left us stuck in our homes without much to do, other than pick up debris from yards and clean.*

For about a week we had no internet either. So, we had to find ways to distract our minds from all the bad news and lack of hope that the government could restore water, power, and phones quickly.

At home, we dusted off our board games, including Game of Life, Trouble, and card games such as Coup and Sleeping Queens. The girls love game time with Michael and me.

Another pastime includes checking in with Grandma. Her home becomes the family command center, where everyone stops by to check in every couple of days. No phones means you better go and check on your love ones in person. At Grandma's, we got out the dominos and the puzzles to keep busy.

Family meals are also a great way to avoid leftovers. Since they don't keep without refrigeration, you must eat it all in one seating. Extended family to the rescue!

This week I also went with my pastor on a walking tour of our church neighborhood to visit with our church members and pray over their families. After which Pastor, her daughter, and I had an adventure driving around fallen posts and electrical lines to make sure other members, who live a bit farther out, knew that we were thinking of them.

And we have also dusted off some reading material to combat boredom. I'm about to finish a novel, "La Casa de la Laguna," by Rosario Ferre. Have a book by news reporter Jorge Ramos lined up for my next reading.

I wonder, "What are other friends doing to entertain their minds during these times?"

Standing in line does not count; that is a necessity, not a pastime.

Staying strong,

Sandra

Standing in line for cash, for food, for gas and for ice is what 50% of the population seemed to be doing in any given day. There is an ice plant near our home. When you live on a tropical island, there is such as business as selling ice.

Whenever you have a party, a field trip, or a group of people working outdoors, you must get at least one bag of ice to keep the drinks cool and the crowd happy. When the power goes out, people bring out their beach coolers and move the essentials from the fridge to the cooler.

After Maria, the choices were: go without refrigeration, run your fridge using a generator, or bring out the coolers. With the whole island without power, many would stand in line for hours to buy one bag of ice at whatever price it was being sold. So, at Rogelio's ice plant in Caguas, the line would start as early as 6:00 a.m., even though they would not start selling ice until about 11:00 a.m. People would bring beach chairs, umbrellas, snacks, and a couple of family members, hoping to get a couple of bags of ice before they ran out.

The ice plant was running on diesel generators, and diesel also became a commodity. Diesel distributors had to choose which clients to bring diesel to and which clients to ignore. The diesel crisis got to the point where the government was taking over diesel trucks and diverting them to the main hospitals in order to keep their generators running. One can only imagine the conflict between supplying paying customers with diesel and supplying a bankrupt government, especially during a crisis. Everyone was putting on pressure and calling in favors.

Our culturally unique expressions of resilience and creativity were
evident even in the lines. We had to laugh when we saw four men
sitting on beach chairs under a canopy playing dominos on a plastic
table, all while waiting in line near a gas station. Others were selling
ice-cold water and other drinks to folks that were waiting. Yet others
were giving away bottled water and snacks to keep those in line from
dehydrating. Some friends sat in their cars for up to eight hours,
waiting to get gasoline.

On the home front, most people were spending lots of hours at
home. Schools were closed. Public schools took over ninety days to
reopen. Some never did. Many buildings, malls, and small businesses
remained closed, due to structural damage, lack of electricity, or
both. For many, it must have felt like house arrest. Not being able to
go anywhere, having little or no money, no entertainment, and the
heat and mosquitoes were driving some people mad. We felt blessed
that our home was relatively safe, our roof was intact except for some
water leaks, and we still had funds to supply our basic needs.

Our habits and the way we spent time changed dramatically. We
found ourselves spending a lot of time on our covered porch
escaping the heat.

Friday September 29, 2017

The green Porch

*It still has not rained since Maria. The temperatures
easily climb into the 90's, and, with the heat index, it
feels like 100 degrees Fahrenheit, which is "fry an egg on
the sidewalk" kind of heat.*

*Under these conditions, we normally stay indoors,
sitting under a fan and drinking ice-cold lemonade or
water. Alternatively, we would escape to some air-
conditioned place like the movie theater.*

But Maria took it all away. There are no fans, no ice, no air conditioning, and, for some, not even a home to go to.

What are we to do? Find the coolest place with shade and avoid most physical activity.

In my case, I've been spending much time on my green porch. When we were house hunting, we felt right at home when we toured this house. It has a long porch on the south side of the house that offers much shade, and a nice breeze runs from front to back most days.

The previous owners added it to the original structure, and it connects to the front porch through an ornate iron gate. The half wall on its side is crowned by more iron grates that offer a partial view of the city on the valley below and the mountains in the background.

The back gate allows the dog to visit the back yard and allows us to carefully observe the birds that live around here, mostly bananaquits and a black bird commonly known as "chango," which looks like a small crow.

These days, we sit on our green patio furniture, put our feet up on the wicker ottoman that used to be red, and wait for hours to pass by while reading, napping, or playing board games.

Lydia (our youngest) likes to run with the dog or ride an old scooter from one end to the other, going under the hammock -- while I'm lying on it!

Several times a day, the green porch gate is opened: to take the dog on a walk, to take the garbage out, or to let the girls out on an adventure exploring the neighborhood.

The kitchen is now partially outside. The BBQ grill is also our stove, so we prepare our heat meals in the alcove that the green porch has by the wall that was built for a half bathroom.

In the late afternoon from the green porch, we wave Hi to our neighbors as we watch the daylight fade and the police cars' blue lights zoom by on Highway 52 not too far away. The curfew is approaching, but cars are still on the roads.

The green porch also serves as a chapel to read the Bible and pray and cry over the many needs of our country and for all who are suffering. It's also a place to think and reflect of a better tomorrow, a day when all this devastation is but a distant memory.

On hot evenings, we bring a lantern out to light up the green porch and play some games or read a bit before going to bed.

And as we lay in bed sweating, we think of tomorrow coming soon to sit out on the green porch with a hot drink at hand to do it all over again.

Staying strong on the porch,

Sandra

Preserving mental health after a crisis, such as natural disaster, is a balancing act. Most people know what to do to keep their bodies healthy, or at least to survive. Our instinct kicks in to preserve our bodies -- to eat, rest, protect ourselves from the elements. But, how do we protect our minds from persistent worry, sorrow, and anxiety?

After Maria, it seemed that all you could find was bad news. People died during the hurricane -- some sixty some lives were lost that day according to the official government count. However, hundreds were missing and hundreds more died in the days and weeks after the hurricane. People could not get their insulin or keep it refrigerated.

Folks in nursing homes or hospital ICUs and people who were bed ridden at home were not able to keep their oxygen, gastric pumps and other equipment running to preserve their lives.

Many who were severely ill died when their treatments were not followed due to the crisis following Maria. The stress of having elderly parents or relatives in those conditions kicked in high gear. And, for those who lost homes and employment during the hurricane, to then have to lose a loved one was too much to bear.

Many Puertorricans sent their elderly parents, sick children and dying relatives to the U.S. soon after Maria, hoping to preserve their lives. But not everyone had family in the U.S. to receive them, or the willingness to leave their home country.

For many who were depressed before Maria, the crisis of being unemployed, homeless, and helpless was too much to overcome. Suicide rates began to rise weeks after the hurricane. When asked by social workers and psychologists, many folks expressed feeling nervous, anxious, and unable to sleep, and some even showed signs of distress whenever it would start raining. Relieving the stress from the hurricane is crucial for many whose mental health was affected by Maria and its aftermath.

One of those who had to be evacuated after Maria was little Sebastian, the son of a family friend. Sebastian was born with congestive heart failure requiring heart surgery. Other health complications and the lack of adequate care on the island delayed his surgery. He had a tracheotomy, and his little life depended on machines and a strict regimen of care. He lived in the hospital after birth for seven-and-a-half months. A month before Maria, Sebastian was sent home from the hospital, still waiting for his surgery.

After Maria, Sebastian's father, a young man named Axel, had to spend his days in lines at gas stations, looking for gasoline to run the generator that was ensuring his son's life.

A few weeks after Maria, an anonymous millionaire joined a U.S. charity to send a personal plane to Puerto Rico filled with medical supplies. On the return flight, the plane transported, free of charge, six families with sick patients, including Sebastian and his family of five.

After a brief stop in an East Coast hospital, Sebastian and his family traveled to Texas, where wonderful people received them with open arms and helped them find a place to live and medical care for him. In January 2018, this precious baby turned one year old. Sebastian and his family are doing well. They are starting from zero in a new country. For them, Maria had a huge price: leaving all their loved ones behind in order to save their baby's life.

Chapter Seven - Hanging by a Thread

I find that one of the ways to keep my spirits up during hard times is to focus on serving others. There is something that happens when we transfer attention to the needs of other people that allows us to see our own reality from a different perspective. During this crisis, it also helped me to write what I was experiencing and how I interpreted those experiences in a type of online diary. My friends online who were reading my updates encouraged me to keep writing, so I did.

September 30, 2017

Hanging by a thread

How many times have I pulled on a thread of a blouse or skirt only to realize that I shouldn't have? I've end up ripping a seam or a hem.

When I read the news of what's happening across our Puerto Rico, it makes me think that most things, people, and systems here have been hanging by a thread for too long.

When 155 mph winds blew by last week, 100% of the country lost power and most lost all communications. Today, eight full days later, only 30% have access to phone lines. Only 40% of banks and ATMs are operational, and about 10% have power.

A few days ago, only 40% of gas stations were operational and about 30% of grocery stores.

And who suffers the most? The poor, the elderly, and those who live paycheck to paycheck, without much cash, without a relative to come and rescue them or buy them a plane ticket to escape the island of lacking.

It's so sad to see the aerial photos that portray signs that read, "SOS we need water and food," or a simple "HELP" engraved on a grass patch.

And it's even sadder to read politicians blaming one another.

It's also sad when the president of the U.S. tweets his venom from afar instead of getting on a plane and coming to look at the despair square in the eye. After all, he had a visit scheduled for this week. But it does not surprise me; an island hanging by a thread is not part of his political agenda right now. What can 3.4 million Puertorricans (U.S. citizens) who are broke do for the great financial interest of a few?

But then I read the reactions of people here who are filled with hope, and it reminds me that, even if our power lines, roads, and financial system were hanging by a thread, our faith has and will be firmly planted on the rock that is Jesus Christ.

And nothing can separate us from the love of God -- not poverty, lack of electricity, lack of effective government, lack of gasoline, or communication. No, nothing can separate us from the love of Jesus Christ our Lord.

Staying strong,

Sandra

PS. It rained today. Thank you God, we needed water!

Driving has always been challenging in Puerto Rico. There are simply too many cars and not enough reliable means for public transportation. Construction and development of commercial areas have made the issue worse. But the worst traffic day in the past does not compare with traffic after Maria.

Every intersection is now a mess of cars trying to go in all different directions at the same time, without traffic lights or traffic cops.

On many occasions, drivers or passengers get out of the cars to direct traffic temporarily in order to unlock an intersection. And some folks have even volunteered to direct traffic on a temporary basis.

Drivers, sick of traffic jams, are so thankful that they even give cash tips to these volunteers, some of whom are unemployed and others perhaps homeless or addicts. It makes me wonder why we didn't think of this sooner, whenever the power goes out or an intersection becomes practically a parking lot during rush hour.

And, yes, before the hurricane, the power used to go out all the time. After moving to the U.S. in 1995, I returned in 2009. Getting our first electric bill in Puerto Rico was a rude awakening. The cost of energy for our tiny two bedroom apartment in the island was twice what we paid in the Chicago suburbs for a three bedroom duplex with central air conditioning. That means that we pay more for energy per kilowatt, but have more power outages and less maintenance than practically any city or town in the U.S.

Monday October 2, 2017

12 days after Maria

Hope

We have a saying in Puerto Rico that says, "Hope is the last thing that one loses." I would have to add to that saying, "...and patience is the first thing that one loses."

I like results. I enjoy being able to finish a task or a project or reach a goal. I love the process of planning and seeing how each step gets me closer to my objective.

I must confess that I'm not very patient, and I hate excuses. I find it hard to understand people who are either pessimists or not action driven. When working on challenging projects, I'd rather be surrounded by people with ingenuity and creativity.

In times of crisis, we don't stop to think if we should fight, flight, or freeze. It just happens; as part of the animal species, we react. In terms of hope, I think I have been granted a large enough dose.

I'm the type of person that will pray for a sick person to get healed while others are praying for God to take them. Last summer, I experienced that up close and personal with a child that drowned. His body was pulled from the water, lips blue, and not breathing. We prayed while first responders administered CPR. God gave life back to that little boy. A few days later he was running around, unharmed.

My hope is not based on my ability, my personality or my upbringing. My hope rests on the supreme source of hope that is Jesus Christ, my rock, my savior. To live for Him and with Him is a very real experience. Each minute that we are alive is because of His mercy, and once we stop breathing, we will live in His presence forever.

In the meantime, God allows us to have the Fruit of the Spirit, which is a nice combo, including patience. Here in Puerto Rico, we will be exercising that patience overtime for the next few months. And we will do so at home, waiting in line, at work, sitting in traffic, at school, dealing with government, with systems, with neighbors, and even with ourselves.

This does not mean that we must tolerate things that are unjust or ignore things that should be denounced, rejected, and protested. However, we must be wise to distinguish between that which is intolerable and what is just inconvenient.

People going hungry or thirsty or the sick dying in hospitals due to the lack of diesel fuel are things that must not be tolerated.

Having to stand in line to buy food, with money in our pockets, is inconvenient. And inconveniences have been multiplied times one hundred on our island. Let us not lose hope; let's harvest patience.

Staying strong,

Sandra

Chapter Eight - Something Stinks

The last time Puerto Rico experienced a hurricane that reached Category Five was perhaps in 1928, during Hurricane San Felipe. Back then, the island was very different. One can only imagine how many people living in the countryside in wooden houses lost all of their belongings and crops.

With modern times come modern problems. Maria left us surrounded by garbage. Homes that flooded were emptied out into streets and sidewalks. Every other street seemed to be littered with furniture, appliances, roofing materials and more. And there were also all the fallen trees that had to be separated so that FEMA would pay for its disposal. And while the government made up their mind on how to collect and, more importantly, how to pay for all the extra garbage collection, the problem of rotting garbage started to stink up the island.

It only got worse once it started raining. Many streets had so much garbage that when it rained, water started accumulating and many neighborhoods flooded. The result: more loss of property, and, in some cases, homes that were starting to recover from Maria were now flooded by rain and sewer waste.

> *Tuesday Oct 3, 2017*
> *13 days since Hurricane Maria*
>
> *It's nasty, ya'll.*
>
> *After nearly two weeks without power, things are rotting everywhere. There is rotten food, dead animals, stagnant water, and people's refrigerators.*
>
> *I thought I had dealt with ours when the power first went out. I thought that all the food was out except a few items and condiments.*

Yesterday, a strong odor alerted me to the contrary. And today, after running errands and checking on some friends we had not heard from, I came home and decided to tackle the beast.

This is the second time in as many weeks that I cleaned the sucker! Just be thankful I didn't post pictures.

I had to pull out the drawers and the glass shelves to get at some strange liquid that looked like soy sauce. I know... yuck! That was not the worst; mildew was starting to form on one corner and there were larvae. I about lost it when I realized tiny eggs were all over between the nooks and crannies of my refrigerator.

It took longer than expected to clean, but I got it all out. And of course we only have water from our tank, so I had to figure out how to do this without wasting water.

It made me think of my life. When something starts going wrong, the longer you wait to deal with it, the bigger it gets. Our hearts, minds and spirits have lots of places where old things can rot and larva can live. We must confess, forgive, stop, and pray before it gets nasty, ya'll.

I just thank God that I didn't wait a few more days. I don't think I would be able to manage worms in my fridge...

Please pray that the water authority here on the island is able to bring many more areas up soon, so that people can have running water and more folks don't get sick.

Staying strong,

Sandra

On any given day, I feel like a reporter on a weird assignment on a made up country where anything goes because the government and local institutions have lost control.

Don't get me wrong -- not all assignments are sad or dangerous. Once we got connected to the Internet, we became aware of all the folks in the U.S. who were looking for their Puertorrican relatives and were unable to contact them.

On social media, people posted pictures of their elderly parents who lived in remote areas and wondered if anyone had news about them. We felt their burden, but in most instances it was like looking for a needle in a haystack.

The first person to ask if we could help someone she knew locate a family member was Ruth, someone we met at church in the U.S. many years ago. When she mentioned the town they lived in, we had to decline to help. It was hard to say no, but the area was a good three hours away in a zone where damage to homes was not as significant. We suspected the relatives were just without a phone and not internet savvy. Given that gasoline was still hard to obtain, we could not embark on such a quest.

The next such request was from our friends, Teresa and Ray, in Florida. Ray had not heard from a great-uncle who lived in our city. With the address and online navigation map, we headed out to look for Uncle Cheo. It turned out he lives in a barrio on the other side of a mountain that we see from our house, on the way to the mountain town of Aguas Buenas.

I figured that this uncle would know our friend, Ray, so I didn't memorize the relationship that Teresa had described in her message. We found Uncle Cheo. He was fine, sitting at home with his wife. As it turned out, they were surrounded by their adult children and other relatives of his wife who lived on the same street.

It was funny that Uncle Cheo and his wife, a sweet lady in her late 70s, had no idea who our friend Ray was, but nevertheless they were thrilled by our visit. We sat on the back porch of their two story humble home and ate some candy they insisted in sharing with us. We heard their hurricane story and observed the damage to the homes in their barrio from their high vantage point.

At this point, every day had the potential of being boring and mundane or a purpose-filled adventure.

Wednesday October 4, 2017

14 days since Maria

Today's adventure included;

1) Attended an insurance orientation to place a claim for our church building's damages.

2) Got four D batteries as a gift from the American Baptist Churches. Badly needed, as our lantern and flashlights run on D batteries and they are nowhere to be found on the island since before Maria. That gift was gold! Thanks ABC!

3) Visited my doctor. His office was open, even though they had no power. He was wearing his shorts and figured out that, since he cannot submit claims to the plan, he would charge $20 per visit, which to me is not that much more than the copay. Now I have my prescription for my meds that ran out.

4) Got chicken on a stick and took it to my mom for lunch. She was bored and welcomed my visit as a good distraction. And she gave me a gallon of drinking water. Bonus!

5) Michael and the girls went grocery shopping at the Amigo in Caguas, and, praise God, they are accepting plastic payments! But they had no bottled water for sale.

6) *Went to check on an elderly couple whose relatives in the U.S. had not heard from and asked if we could do a wellness check-up. They had no idea who our friends in the U.S. were, distant great-nephew, but they were happy to have visitors and asked us to come by any time. They live in a humble community nestled in the mountains of our city, on the other side of some hills that we see from our porch. We had never visited their neighborhood.*

7) *Gasoline ahoy! On the way back from visiting the elderly couple, we saw a gas station open with a very short line. We were in and out in eight minutes!!! And we were able to buy drinking water! Lines these days are taking between thirty minutes to two hours; this line was nothing, piece of cake.*

8) *The girls were begging for a treat, so we stopped at the only Wendy's in town that seems to be open and got Frosties. They only had vanilla, and there was no ice for drinks. Also, they had no hamburger nor buns. So we had a baked potato and chicken nuggets with our ice cream. Not as weird as the pancakes with canned corn beef we had for breakfast! With no refrigeration you must eat things while they are still good, regardless of the time of day.*

9) *Finally, on the way home we saw a city water tanker near our neighborhood filling up people's empty containers. There is hope! Our home water tank ran out yesterday; now we most import our washing water.*

Lines at banks are the longest. We pray that more and more stores can get their systems online, so that people won't need to do all-cash transactions, and the bank lines will go down.

We also pray that the water authority can get more people water at home. That would mean one less trouble, especially for the sick and elderly who cannot be carrying big containers of water.

Today was a good day.

Staying strong,

Sandra

When I was young girl, my family moved from Chicago to Puerto Rico. In great contrast with Chicago, the island offered my father few job prospects. The first couple of years after returning to his homeland, Dad took whatever jobs he could get, and we lived wherever we could rent. My dad sold disposable cups, worked at a pizzeria, took a tour guide class, and ran a little corner store where candy and cold drinks were sold to people in the neighborhood and church-goers after Sunday service.

Dad eventually landed a job as a guard at the Bacardi rum distillery just west of San Juan. The job offered stability and good pay, but it was far from our home and he worked nights. This is why my parents welcomed the opportunity to move to Toa Baja, about ten miles from Dad's new job. There was a catch -- the new place was an empty lot on land that some 100 families had invaded. So, we were offered the chance to own a home, but in order to do so, we had to become squatters. My mom's father and her brothers pitched in and helped my Dad build a small wooden house with tin roofing in our plot by the canal.

The year was 1973, and the place was called Ingenio, named after the old sugar cane processing site in Toa Baja. Basic services were reduced to a community faucet down the street. There was no electricity, no sewer, no water, no street lights, nothing. It was nobody's land, and we moved in when Alvin was six years old, I was four, and little Carlitos was a baby.

My mother remembers moving in her appliances but not being able to use the refrigerator, the washing machine, or the toaster. My dad got ahold of an inverter that they would hook to the car battery so they could turn on a lamp in the house at night. Dad worked nights sometimes, so when he was gone, we were left with a couple of oil lamps to fight the absolute darkness.

We had no working toilet at first. There was an outhouse in the back that we shared with the neighbors. And nobody in their right mind would use it at night, so we had a couple of chamber pots under our beds that were used at night and emptied in the morning.

At first, we had to carry water from the only faucet down the street, but soon the neighbors started connecting recycled PVC pipes first to the home closest to the faucet, then from there to the neighbor's, and on and on until it got to our home, six or seven houses away.

Mom hand washed our clothes, and the sun was the dryer. If we wanted a warm bath, my mother would warm up water on the gas stove, and we would use a cup to draw water from a plastic basin in the shower. We slept under mosquito nets to avoid the mosquitoes, which were vicious given our proximity to the canal. Mosquito nets look sort of like tents, and they are made out of tulle. You hang each end from the walls over the beds and tuck the edges under the mattress.

Sleeping under the mosquito nets was the one time at night when you were safe from insects flying into your face, including flying roaches. Mom said that living for about nine months under those conditions with three small children was hard, but it also made her stronger. You see, my mother is a fighter -- she never quits and never accepts defeat.

After Maria, some of my female cousins who live in the U.S. were concerned about my mom. They invited Mom to go visit with them for a while. I'm sure some of them could not understand why Mom was in her home and had not moved in with me. What they didn't get is that I was in the same situation, except there were four of us at our house, so Mom was more comfortable in her own home. I knew that Mom was not going to let inconveniences push her into accepting defeat. After all, she had lived all of it before, with fewer resources, and she knew it would be temporary.

Thursday Oct 5, 2017

15 days since Hurricane Maria

Normally, when fifteen days have passed, an event is no longer news, unless it is a catastrophe or events of significance continue to unfold, enough to grab the curiosity of a large audience.

Today it has been fifteen days since Maria. Some things look like they are back to normal; others are far from normal.

Like when I stepped into my local pharmacy to buy some medication, the place had AC, lights were on, kids were buying cold drinks and candy. And the pharmacy even had their computers up and running.

However, traffic was a mess. At 1:00 p.m., the gridlock made it feel like 6:00 p.m. on a Friday. And to see some civilians taking over the role of traffic cops was anything except normal.

Today, we were on a mission to get some water and do some laundry. Our laundry baskets were full of dirty clothes. Some of us were running out of clean clothes, and we had less than a gallon of water in the whole house.

Thanks to the fact that we have cell phone signal in our area, I was able to get ahold of my good friend, Olga. Her part of town has running water. She welcomed our whole family into her home, not only to take showers but also to do two loads of laundry... by hand.

It was a team effort: washing, rinsing, wringing, and packing, all while one member of the family took a turn taking a nice shower. And, in the meantime, my friend and her daughter filled our empty containers with clean, potable water for us to take home. Water is as precious as gasoline right now.

Something funny happened. As we arrived at her house with our mission "get clean" in mind, it started raining hard.

The first two five-gallon containers we use to wash were filled by rain water coming down a gutter near her laundry room.

That reminded me that all water comes from God, and he gave us so much of it that in a matter of minutes we had collected ten gallons and enough to wash and rinse our first set of clothes.

God gives sun and rain to all, regardless of our behavior or worthiness. Even though it's hard for us to understand, the world does not revolve only around us and whatever crisis we are experiencing. Which, by the way, in other countries is their version of "normal."

Today, I thank God for rain, for my faithful friend Olga, and for selfless people, like the lady who volunteered to direct traffic outside the mall at the busy street crossing.

By the way, that afternoon rain also means that tonight we can sleep better, without the humidity and heat we have had for the past week. Thank you God for the rain!

Staying strong,

Sandra

At this point, the lack of water had become a problem for everyone. At home, our toilets turned into latrines. It takes two to three gallons to flush a toilet, or more if you want to do it properly with enough clean water left in it afterwards. Keeping three toilets clean was nearly impossible, so we started using the one toilet near the girls' rooms. That bathroom has the best ventilation. We minimized the flushing to a few times a day. It was nasty.

Meanwhile, through the island a potential epidemic of leptospirosis was feared. Leptospirosis is an infection caused by the leptospira bacteria mainly carried by rats' urine and transferred to humans and domestic animals.

Many of the symptoms are similar to the flu, but in some cases it can cause kidney failure, bleeding of the lungs, meningitis, and even death.

Apparently, the bacteria thrives in warm and wet environments, and experts say that it abounds in rivers after heavy rain falls. Dozens of people were showing up at hospitals, especially in the northeast towns, with leptospirosis symptoms. Doctors were not sure if folks were getting infected by having contact with the rivers while bathing and washing clothes; or if they were ingesting it from contaminated streams and springs that, for many, were the only source of water. This is the last thing we needed: an epidemic that threatened the lives of the millions of survivors who were working to overcome the humanitarian crisis we were experiencing after the hurricane.

Saturday Oct 7th

17 days since Hurricane Maria

A week or so ago, I posted an invitation to anyone interested in helping families affected by Hurricane Maria to contact me or simply send a check to my address.

I committed to pass on 100% of donations to people in need, especially those who lost their home.

I had no idea what kind of response I would get, but within days I had heard from four people.

One of those was a dear friend that I met when I lived in Chicago. She has a great heart, but also good brains. She asked many good questions and helped me consider ways I could best go about spreading the donations among those in need. She also helped me find a way to get the funds delivered to me faster.

Then she found some other friends wanting to help and even a matching donor, so her gift doubled.

My heart melted when she told me the amount she had deposited into my account.

Today I started the fun part of the process, handing out donations, because I truly believe that it is more blessed to give than to receive. When I saw the home of this precious family, how it was missing the whole roof and all their belongings scattered and damaged, it made me think that, even if the gift we were giving them was not large enough to recover what they had lost, it would at least be enough to let them know that they are not alone or forgotten.

I will not post pictures of the people we are helping or their homes, out of respect, but I will share the pictures with those that donated. And I will keep records of the gifts.

Tomorrow, we'll get to visit another family who will receive a check. And I cannot wait until all the funds are used up.

If you wish to join my little campaign, let me know. I can keep going as far as you will send me. Send me a message or leave a comment.

This week I was reading the book of Joel, which was kind of depressing until I got to Chapter 2. I especially liked verses 21-27:

"Don't be afraid, O land. Be glad now and rejoice, for the Lord has done great things.

"Don't be afraid, you animals of the field, for the wilderness pastures will soon be green. The trees will again be filled with fruit; fig trees and grapevines will be loaded down once more.

"Rejoice, you people of Jerusalem! Rejoice in the Lord your God! For the rain he sends demonstrates his faithfulness. Once more the autumn rains will come, as well as the rains of spring.

"The threshing floors will again be piled high with grain, and the presses will overflow with new wine and olive oil.

"The Lord says, 'I will give you back what you lost to the swarming locusts, the hopping, the stripping locusts, and the cutting locusts. It was I who sent this great destroying army against you.'

"Once again you will have all the food you want, and you will praise the Lord your God, who does these

miracles for you. Never again will my people be disgraced.

"Then you will know that I am among my people Israel that I am the Lord your God, and there is no other. Never again will my people be disgraced."[1]

Some of the many words that God gave Joel for Israel resonate in our hearts this week. From the autumn rains, to the promise of trees with fruit (we lost most our agriculture in one day), to the foods we want (now missing from the store shelves). God even promises to redeem our dignity, after being teased and ridiculed by the U.S. President during his visit, those words are timely. I hear the words "never again will my people be disgraced" as a promised to my land and my people.

It's great to see people in the U.S. collecting food and water to send to Puerto Rico. That emergency humanitarian aid is great. Even churches here have collected help and delivered it to those in need.

However, we must think long term. Forty dollars' worth of groceries only goes as far as feeding a person for a few days. Folks need to pay for gas, lunch money for their kids, repairs to their homes, medication, and their phone bill. Some people will not have work until the electricity is restored to their places of business. Some people need to buy even water to drink, because none is coming out of the faucet.

In the meantime, please pray. Pray for the poor who need the most help. Pray for water to be restored to all communities soon. Pray for schools and businesses to

---

[1] Joel 2:21-27 Holy *Bible*, New Living Translation, copyright © 1996, 2004, 2007, 2013, 2015 by Tyndale House Foundation.

open up again, so people can get back to a paying job. Pray for the government to be more efficient, faster, and farther reaching. And pray for us, the people of God, to do our jobs well, helping, loving, being a blessing.

Staying strong,

Sandra

This was probably the most exciting assignment so far. I was convinced that God was allowing us to live the promise expressed by Paul in his letters to the Romans. Chapter 8, verse 28 is my favorite passage from scripture: "And we know that all things work together for good to them that love God, to them who are the called according to his purpose."[2]

Sometimes people question why I moved back to Puerto Rico in 2009. To many, it didn't make sense that I was leaving behind a home, a job, and a country filled with opportunities to come live in a country that was going down the drain, fast. Some of our friends in the U.S. felt like we were abandoning them, and they didn't understand why, either. And my own family, although happy, seemed perplexed by our choice to move here.

My husband and I have always striven to be where God calls us to be, not where we would rather be. It's hard to understand, because in human terms it does not make sense. But, after living by faith, we know that we would rather be where God calls us and not where we are comfortable. Because, when you are in the right location, you can see what God is doing and be part of it. Instead of concentrating on what makes you "happy" or "successful," you can experience the amazing truth of what it is to be content in God's presence and to do His will.

After Maria, when our friends and relatives generously started opening their checkbooks and sending us money, we knew that we

---

[2] Romans 8:28 King James Version (KJV) Public Domain.

were being part of something that had been orchestrated by God long before the hurricane was ever formed.

We got donations from cousins and in-laws, but also from people we had not seen or spoken to in five, six, ten years even. Friends that we met when I was doing my Master's Degree in 1998, people whom we went to church with in 2000, the father or a friend whom we had only met once at a wedding back in 2004, ladies who were friends with Michael's mother, and people whom we had never met. They all pitched in to help Puertorricans in need.

At first we were overwhelmed by the need. There were hundreds of thousands of people in need. Whom should we help? So, we decided to concentrate on people who lost their roofs and those whose homes were flooded. We were hearing the stories of how FEMA emergency funds were not being delivered swiftly and how not everyone had access to emergency housing, aid, food, etc.

Next, we determined that the amount should be significant. We could give many people $25, but that would have little effect. So, instead, we would give amounts over $500 to as many folks as we could.

The most satisfying aspect of this operation was to see the responses of those who received the help. It was like they received an injection of hope. There were many tears of joy that fell on my cheeks as we went about the distribution of the donations. We were handing out money, but they were receiving much more than that. They were receiving the hope that things would get better, the feeling of solidarity and that someone cared. Someone remembered. God remembered them!

> *October 9, 2017*
>
> *19 days since Maria*
>
> *Today's chores/status updates*
>
> *1) Girls went back to school. They seemed happy to recover some kind of normal routine. They lost a few*

classmates whose families relocated to the States due to the crisis post hurricane. Traffic was bad.

2) I attempted to pay our health insurance bill, with no luck. Their system cannot handle plastic yet. Will go back with a check later this week.

At least they told me the policy will not be cancelled due to late payment. Traffic was bad.

3) I went grocery shopping. On the way there, I got hungry. Line outside the store was long, slow-moving, and in the sun. I knew I would not handle that situation well, so I left. Traffic was bad.

4) I remembered I had a lollipop in my purse, so I ate it while trying to get out of the mall. Then I saw a rare but welcome scene: a traffic cop at the light and across from the entrance to another grocery store. Traffic finally moved.

5) The second store was in a less crowed mall, and the line was in the shade. The sugar of the lollipop worked, and I knew I could handle the fifteen-minute line, no problem. And, voila, they told me their system was working. Nevertheless, I shopped carefully, in case I had to pay cash. There was plenty of some products, like bread, but still shortages of others, like fruit, veggies, disposable plates, and meats, and this particular store had completely ran out of drinking water. Yet this was the first successful errand today. It gave me hope that I could go on.

6) Next on my list was to get a hot lunch for me and Michael Richter. I was thinking tacos when rain started falling so hard that I knew I would get drenched if I attempted to stop at the taco place, plus, you guessed it, traffic was bad.

7) Went home and made turkey sandwiches with the deli meat I had just bought. Since we only run our gas generator around eight hours a day, our refrigeration is not constant, and we need to be careful about what we buy and how long we keep it. Turkey was a nice change from tuna!

8) I went out to pick up the girls earlier than usual, given the traffic situation.

Without street lights, main streets get grid-locked, and a twenty-minute drive can easily double. However, this time, it was also raining. It rained so hard that when I got to about a block from leaving our neighborhood, I saw a man crossing the street in waist-deep water. Debris and leaves from the hurricane had most likely blocked street drains, and there was a little lake on the busy road. Thankfully, there was an alternate route not too far away. Little did I know that, on the way to school, I would encounter not one but two small lakes. I was able to pass with care and while praying, "Please God don't let the water in my car. Help me cross." I was forty minutes late to pick up the girls, which gave the rain enough time to ease up. And, no, water did not get into my car, but traffic was bad.

9) Can you do one more errand? OK. Since Friday, we had been looking for a service that would come to the house and fill up our reserve water tank. It's a huge (600 gallons) tank that sits on our house, and, when the water is out (happens often here), the whole house uses the water in the tank automatically. A pump pushes the water out of the tank with enough pressure to reach all areas of our home. Since the hurricane, we have had no electricity. This means water from the tank was coming down just by gravity with very low pressure. That probably helped the water last for about fifteen days. After one provider who could not guarantee a delivery time and another with more competitive pricing, I came home today to see a van with a water tank inside and a hose connected to our tank. There was one tiny problem: the pump he had was not strong enough, even though we were powering it with our gas generator! So, the guy said he will come back tomorrow with a stronger pump. At least he did fill up our empty buckets before he left.

So, yeah, today was full of dead ends, or so it seems. Life is a never-ending series of quests, tasks, dreams, and attempts. We must persevere, last, keep going, cherish the progress, learn from mistakes, and pray a lot that water does not flood our engines.

I used to think that when something bad happened to me, I did not deserve it. I also used to think that, if I was doing God's will, things should go well for me. I thought things like that were unfair. Now I have come to understand that life is not fair and that good and bad things happen to everyone. I know that every good and perfect gift comes from above, from the Father of Lights, who is God. However, good gifts are more than material things, even more than good things like running water and smooth traffic. Good gifts are deeper, like patience, perseverance, goodness, kindness, love, and contentment.

I strive to say, like Paul, "I've learned to be content in abundance or when lacking..."

Staying strong,

Sandra

Chapter Nine - Some Stay, Some Go

During the aftermath of Maria, many Puertorricans were faced with the difficult decision of whether or not to leave the island, either temporarily or permanently.

We all lost family members, classmates, neighbors, coaches, teachers, co-workers, doctors and friends to the mass migration that followed the hurricane.

On social media, some started having strong reactions to those who were leaving. Those who left responded with equally strong arguments.

There are practical implications for those of us who stayed. We would be left to rebuild a country with a smaller tax base, less resources, fewer brains, and fewer hands. And, let's face it, it's depressing to see people leave when you stay behind in very hard, if not deplorable, conditions.

The Puertorricans who moved (mostly to the US) had practical implications to consider as well. Many were penniless, unable to cope with the lack of resources, others were unemployed, and many were just sick and tired of not being able to find a means to move forward with their careers, health treatments, and living conditions.

> *Monday Oct 16, 2017*
>
> *It's been 26 days since Hurricane Maria. Some schools and universities are back in session. Many companies and businesses have opened their doors again, but there are many businesses that still cannot operate fully.*
>
> *Some, like food trucks, have increased their hours of operation. They were not dependent on electricity or water before, given the nature of their business. Once they were able to get supplies, many reopened and have been at it like never before.*

Others have re-invented their offerings, focusing on products that are in more demand, from washboards for hand washing to battery operated gadgets, and even simple things like cold drinks at street lights or at the line outside ice plants.

And yet many others without savings, homes, jobs or prospects have left the island. In most cases, family members or friends have invited them to take shelter in their homes in the U.S.

To stay or to go? That is the question of many, but it is not an easy decision by any means.

Considerations include;

Extended family - Many feel responsible for their elderly parents or other relatives. If they leave, who would look after them?

Property - Who would buy/rent their property now? How will they maintain their homes, animals, and land? Of course, considerations vary greatly. Those who lost both home and job have nothing more to lose now.

No Plan - Leaving under these circumstances for many means that there is no time to land a job, find schools, or doctors or to decide how to best meet the needs of all family members elsewhere. Some people cannot handle the uncertainty of leaving the familiar, even when staying has its own share of uncertainty.

Commitment - some are deeply committed, invested personally in their communities, churches, jobs, and businesses. For them, getting out now is out of the question. It would be like selling their stocks when the price has significantly dropped, at a great personal and emotional loss.

Support - For others, their whole family and support circle are here, on the island. And, for better or worse, they are rooted in this country and have nobody to welcome them anywhere else.

I was talking the other day with a young electrician. I mentioned that, with the thousands of homes using gas generators and the need to hook them up to homes' main power boxes, he was probably very busy. He agreed and then surprised me by telling me he, too, was leaving the country in a few weeks.

It turned out that his wife, who has a PhD in education, runs a beauty salon. When he ran the numbers on how much it would cost them to run her business on gasoline instead of our already expensive electric power, her business would lose money. Since they need two incomes to raise their family of four, they decided to move to the States. There, his wife can probably land a job teaching and his children can go to public school, saving them hundreds of dollars a month.

So when people ask me if we are moving back to the U.S., it makes me wonder if they assume that it is an easy decision. We have a home here, a church, girls in school, a dog, extended family, a soccer team, a music team, friends, and a community in which we have been investing for eight years. Leaving this investment now seems a little bit like declaring bankruptcy.

If the Lord leads us in a different direction, we are willing to be obedient, but for now we are...

Staying Strong,

Sandra

P.S. For all of those who have chosen to leave or are thinking of leaving, that is your right, and my thoughts above are in no way a criticism. Everyone is doing what they consider best for their family under this horrible situation that we are facing. Godspeed, and may he pave your way!

These days, our visits with friends and family all follow the same pattern. We are so happy to see each other. After all, many lost their lives during or shortly after Maria. Then we talk about the day of the hurricane, we share our "war stories," and finally we talk about the aftermath and the issues we still face and how we best handle them.

It's a group therapy of sorts. Some were traumatized by it and have a hard time moving on to any other subject. Others are pretty much looking forward to moving on with their lives and forgetting the hurricane like it was a nightmare.

I have noticed that most people seem to feel better after you listen to them and validate their experience.

The consensus among my friends in Puerto Rico was that we'd rather have no electricity but have water than the other way around. We can always manage to find substitutes for electricity, like batteries, generators, or inverters, or just go without electricity altogether. Water, on the other hand, is vital.

My daughters, Michael, and I were becoming experts at water conservation -- short showers, water recycling, minimized house cleaning, and many other tricks we came up with to make our water reservoir last. Since the water in the cistern tank above the house only lasted fifteen days after the hurricane, once it was refilled, we were counting the days when we would have city water back again.

I remember the ordeal of filling the cistern. It was ridiculously difficult. First we had to identify a provider, as most of the island was in the same situation, and private water carriers are not the norm. The few that were out there were hard to come by and expensive.

I found a guy online who normally has a drone photography business but apparently was branching out into water distribution for the time being. He was impossible to pin down, was too busy, and kept changing his potential arrival day. Then I saw a sign on the front gate of our neighborhood. I called the number, and the guy was cheaper and available, so I asked him to come and sell us three hundred gallons of water. He arrived, but his pump was not strong enough to get the water all the way to the tank on top of our house. He called around and figured that he needed to buy a new, stronger pump. He left with the promise of getting a pump and returning the next day, but never did.

At this point, we were getting desperate. Carrying water every day and pouring most of it down the toilet was getting old, fast. I was afraid of hurting my back lifting buckets of water each day. So, when I saw a tanker coming into our street, I went and talked to the shady-looking character that was driving it and asked if he would come to my house next. At first, he claimed he was booked for the rest of the evening and gave me his number. About forty-five minutes later, he was in front of my house and, during a nasty rain storm, had his employee climb a ladder up to our roof. The cost per gallon was fifty cents, and the way he figured the measurement was by timing it -- I think it was one hundred gallons every fifteen minutes. Normally, we pay about $40 a month for water, and I'm sure we use way more than six hundred gallons a month.

We paid $200 cash for about four hundred gallons of water in our tank. What else could we do? We were desperate. Shortly after the water guy left, we noticed that the water would not come out of our faucet. We knew he had poured water in the tank, because Michael had checked. He wasn't scamming us; something was wrong.

My brother Alvin came to the rescue. Alvin and Michael tried every trick in the book to get the water to come out of the tank, but it was all in vain. Ah, the frustration of those days was really trying our patience, to the point of losing it all.

We thought it could be that sediments from the empty tank had flowed into the pipe at the end of the system, clogging it, so we had lots of water, but no way of getting out of the tank. The next day, we had our gasoline generator connected to the house's main electrical panel. This allowed us to turn on the pump of the water tank and, *voilá*, water came out of the faucet. It was all a matter of having enough pressure.

So, fast forward a week later, and now water from the city was coming to our house. Our home is on a slope of a mountain, so it took us longer than the rest of the valley to get water, but, when we did, it was such as relief. One less thing for us to worry about.

Oct 17, 2017

Update - We got water today! There is water coming from the faucet!!! This is cause for joy and celebration. Our water tank is again full (600 gallons) and we won't have to pay fifty cents a gallon to fill it. Not sure how long we will have service, but for now, this is great news.

Clean laundry, flushed toilets, and we can even wash our dog now. Poor Sugar, he is looking beige instead of white.

Chapter Ten - What Do We Do with All this Money?

I felt very responsible for the funds that we received from our friends in the U.S. for the hurricane victims. On one hand, there is so much need all around us. On the other hand, if we give away the money to the first person we come in contact with, there will be nothing left when we run into someone who needs it more.

When faced with this dilemma, I think of David who wrote in Psalm 121, "I look up to the mountains—does my help come from there? My help comes from the Lord, who made heaven and earth!" [3] God gives me the wisdom that I don't claim to possess. He places people in my path for a reason, and he reveals their needs.

Friday October 20th

Second Update on Aid Status

It's been 30 days since Hurricane Maria hit our island, destroying homes, agriculture, and businesses and tearing up our electrical grid, our water supply, and, in many cases, people's dreams, too.

I am so thankful to our friends and family in the U.S. who have sent cash donations.

Today, I want to share with you the story of the latest two families that received a check.

The first one was a family made up of a mom, dad, and two teenage boys. She is a cleaning lady, and her husband works for a waste management company. With hard work and sacrifice, they built a concrete house on top of her mother's house. The roof was made of tin panels, as concrete was out of their budget. The night of

---

[3] *Psalm 121:1-2 Holy Bible,* New Living Translation, copyright © 1996, 2004, 2007, 2013, 2015 by Tyndale House Foundation.

*the hurricane, they had boarded up their windows and
tied down the house, including the roof, with cables.
That is a common practice here for that type of
structure. The winds started before they expected and
then a tree fell on their house. A huge Mango tree had
fallen on their roof and part of it blocked their only exit.
Dad and older son managed to move part of the tree
and sort of carved an exit. They escaped and are all fine,
but their house and belongings suffered great damage.
Mom and dad are back to work. Kids go back to school
next week. They are all living in grandma's tiny house.
Dad is trying to fix the house as fast as he can. Their
front yard was filled with dead trees. Their carport was
gone. Mom thanks us for the check. She was so happy.
She said, "I have no words to thank you."*

*The second family is a single woman and foster mother
who lost her roof. She has been living at a shelter for a
month now. She is a pastor (not currently leading a
church). The organization that runs the shelter
appointed her as shelter director, as they know her and
her leadership qualities well. For thirty days, she has
been helping others, when she herself needed rescuing.
Today, she sounded tired and desperate on the phone.
When she got the check, she was speechless; she was on
the way to the bank to beg for a loan. She is a woman of
faith, and she was shocked by how quickly God
answered today's prayer for funds. I think thirty days
with nothing was long enough, don't you? Not a single
aid she has requested had been granted, not even
FEMA's. But God came to the rescue, through people
like you.*

We received $200 this week, in addition to the previous donations. We are committed to keep looking for folks whose homes were severely affected and who lost all or most of their homes. Thank you for your generosity!

Out of respect, we are not posting the pictures of these families or their homes. If you see the news, you have seen the path of destruction that Maria left. It's everywhere you look here.

At home, we are doing fine. We had running water for a whole day, which allowed us to fill our reserve tank. The gas generator that my brother got us and shipped from the U.S. has been working fine. We run it a few hours twice a day to keep our food from spoiling and to run the water pump. It's also very nice to be able to read at night with real lights and every now and then run a coffee maker or a fan. The girls are back to school and we are all healthy, praise God!

Our church is meeting twice a week, daytime services only. We took all the plastic screens off the windows and have managed now without A/C or sound system for a month. It's hard with all the street noises, but we are glad to have a church building with a roof!

It's been a month and we are still...

Staying Strong,

Sandra and family

Chapter Eleven - Who Can Help Us Now?

Among the positive consequences the hurricane brought us was the reconnecting with friends abroad with whom we had lost touch. Such was the case of my friend, Wilma. We met when we were teens. She lived with her parents and three siblings in the mountains of Barranquitas. Her humble heart and great sense of humor quickly attracted many easy friendships.

I remember visiting her church for a day-long event the youth of the region hosted each year. At some point, I went to Wilma's home to take a quick shower and change prior to the evening service. I don't recall how it happened, but Wilma, her three siblings, and I all ended up wearing white that night. I still recall the photo we took, all five of us, a couple of years apart each. They all became my friends that night.

About four years later, in the early 90s, Wilma and I found each other again. This time we were housemates in Green Lake, Wisconsin. We both had applied for a job as summer staff at a Christian retreat center. It was a great summer for all the staffers.

We were young people from all over the U.S., a couple of international students, and three other Puertorricans in addition to Wilma and I. Our friendship deepened that summer in Wisconsin. Little did I know that we were meant to meet again.

Wilma and her family didn't return to Puerto Rico after that summer in Wisconsin. Instead, they all moved to Chicago. In 1995, I took a leave from work to spend a couple of weeks in Chicago with my aunt Mary, who had been diagnosed with cancer and was recovering from surgery and chemotherapy.

I had visited my aunt a couple of times, including one whole summer in 1982. My impression of Chicago was that it was a huge gray city, not a place I was interested in residing. But those two weeks as a young adult, seen through the eyes of my friend Wilma, changed my perspective and allowed me to give Chicago a second chance.

Later that year, with my aunt Mary recovered from her treatment, I quit my job in Puerto Rico and moved in with my aunt.

I spent almost two years working at various odd jobs in Chicago, getting ready to enter university to obtain a graduate degree. That was a period of many happy memories with Wilma and her siblings. We were all young adults, attending the same church, hanging out almost every weekend.

Once I returned from Michigan, where I had gone to do my Master's, Wilma and I ran in different circles, lived in different cities, and were no longer inseparable. So, when she reached out to me after Hurricane Maria, it was a nice surprise. The last time we had seen each other was on Memorial Day, 2014, when our family took a vacation in Chicago and got together with her family and church friends for a barbeque.

This time, Wilma was reaching out to me on behalf of the mega church she attended. Since our single days in Chicago, she had married, and both her and her husband had become members of a rather large church. A leader of her church, Tim (not his real name), approached her to see about coordinating efforts to send aid to Puerto Rico.

Sitting at home, without power, with the aid funds running out, the thought of helping coordinate distribution of aid was very exciting and quite humbling.

In the media, we would read about all the super stars like Marc Antony and Jennifer Lopez collecting millions to help the victims in Puerto Rico. Of course, having lived through similar situations, we knew that not all those funds would reach the needy, or at least not in the most immediate and effective way.

A few days later, I ended up emailing with Tim, and it turned out that they had earmarked $25,000 to help Puerto Rico. Wow! $25,000 that was way more than the $4,060 that we had been able to distribute so far.

Tim and I discussed the next steps. We were to submit three ideas on how to use the funds, and they would pick one idea to back up with their funds. I thought about this for a couple of days and called a good friend of the family, Roberto.

Roberto was the leader of a major Christian denomination on the island and had over eight years of experience coordinating efforts with hundreds of churches. When I called him, he was actually busy distributing food through churches with funds sent by the denominational offices in the U.S. Roberto was very helpful, as he had been submitting proposals and had several projects lined up, waiting for funds to roll them out.

I emailed Tim and shared the ideas with him. He promised to get back to us after meeting with the committee in charge of the Puerto Rico relief fund. I followed up, given that he didn't get back to me after the meeting. He mentioned that one of the projects resonated with the committee and that the meeting was attended by an American missionary lady that had been to Puerto Rico many times through her life.

The next step was to submit a complete proposal. I figured the more information we could provide on how the denomination would be fiscally responsible to them, the better. Roberto sent me the proposal format and -- surprise, surprise -- it was in Spanish. I spent the next couple of days translating it and checking the facts. We included the names of individuals that would be assisted, photos of the damage to their homes, and a well-planned strategy to help over one hundred people with mental health services to prevent burnout of leaders who were in the front lines helping victims.

What happened next was disappointing, to say the least. On each communication with Tim, he would introduce a new piece of information not previously mentioned. So, first he said that the committee decided to fund an idea brought by the missionary lady to repair the dining hall at a camp in the mountains of Adjuntas. So, just like that, $15,000 went to the camp. Then they decided to send the remaining $10,000 to a pastor that was asking for help for the members of his congregation, even though he had lost his own home.

So, it went from wanting to get three ideas to pick one, to picking none of our ideas. Ironically, the pastor whom they chose to fund was one of the individuals that we had wanted to help with our proposal. Three months later, the $10,000 had yet to be sent to that local pastor.

I'm sure I was not the only one getting rejected on proposals to large organizations for worthy projects. However, in the midst of the greatest natural catastrophe in my country in my lifetime, it was sad to lose a grant due to personal relationships or conflicts within a committee. Having the best intentions does not prevent a person or organization from falling into the traps of politics and power plays.

But not everything was bad news. There were Christians whose impact was felt in very tangible ways and fairly quickly. That is how our friend Michelle ended up visiting Puerto Rico for the second time in less than a year.

Michelle was only a girl when Michael met her and her family in his Chicago Humboldt Park neighborhood back in the 80s. Her mom, Lucy, was a Puertorrican born in Chicago who had only visited Puerto Rico once in her life. Michelle always wanted to visit, but her dream didn't come true until she was an adult. Her and her husband came on vacation with their two boys and Lucy less than a year before the hurricane.

During that visit, they came through Caguas, our city, and visited with us for an afternoon. We had dinner and showed them around a bit through Plaza Palmer. At least part of Lucy's family was originally from Caguas, so they were excited to get to visit and learn more about the city their ancestors came from.

Michelle is a brave woman. She has overcome adversity in her life and was not afraid to come back to the island when her pastor organized a trip shortly after Maria. Their church owns a building in

Chicago that used to be a warehouse. After having owned the warehouse for about five years, the church decided it was time to convert the facilities into something more useful. God, however, had his own plans, as it turned out.

The Puertorrican community in Chicago, like in many other U.S. cities, started collecting humanitarian aid to send the island almost immediately after Maria. People opened their hearts and their wallets and aid started arriving at the doors of the non-for-profit organization that had organized the efforts. However, they had no room for all the food and other items that they had received.

That is when someone phoned Pastor Zayas, from Michelle's church, and asked if they could use their facilities to store all the goods. And he was pleased to help. After all, his congregation had many ties to the Puertorrican community, as many of his members are of Puertorrican descent. Pastor Zayas was only too happy to open the doors of his warehouse. He and his wife organized their congregation, and soon pallets filled with water, food, and tarps, and other items were being piled up at their warehouse.

Partnerships continued to form. Someone reached out to the Rainbow Push Coalition, the organization led by Rev. Jesse Jackson. They then reached out to their contacts, and, in the end, a Fedex plane was lined up to transport the aid to Puerto Rico free of charge.

Aid stranded at ports, containers filled with food sitting on the San Juan docks, lack of transportation, and plenty of blame were the trademarks of our government's response. Unable to step up distribution and transportation, their logistics were a mess. At that point, FEMA was not faring any better. They had their own mess with lack of sufficient personnel, no efficient way to communicate, and no blue tarps, since their latest contractor was a flop.

Pastor Zayas, Michelle, and another man from their church came to Puerto Rico to oversee the distribution of all the aid. Working hand in hand with ministries and organizations on the island, the trio traveled through many towns and cities, overseeing the distribution.

Things ran smoothly, given that they relied on locals, who knew what they were doing and had logistics planned in order to avoid chaos. They even finished their scheduled visits one day in advance, which gave them some time to visit friends and family. Each member of their trio picked a home to visit. Michelle contacted us via Facebook, which was the most efficient way to communicate at that point, and we gladly sent her directions to our home.

What happened next was very sweet. After a month and a day of dealing with the hurricane aftermath, aid came to our doorstep. One of the things that was still hard to come by was drinking water. Michelle and the team got up early that Saturday and beat the line at a Costco to bring us water, nonperishable food items and other goodies.

Up to this point, no one had come to our home to offer us any help. On the contrary, we had been coordinating help for others. We considered ourselves pretty blessed. Our home was standing, we had a gas generator, and our cars were running fine. We figured that the humanitarian aid that the government was distributing at the emergency centers should go to people with little to no resources who needed it more than we did. We were fine, or so we thought.

When the team made it to our home that day, we served them coffee, and, as we sat and visited, we told them our Maria survival story. They shared with us what they found in other towns, especially up in the mountains, where landslides had blocked roads and the rain had washed out bridges. Getting to some areas would take hours of driving up roads flanked by fallen trees and electric posts.

When they left, I realized that I had needed that visit. It was important for me to share my pain with someone that was not suffering more than me. As Pastor Zayas told us the story of their church building and how it had been empty for over five years, not being used for their intended purpose due to unexpected obstacles, it became clear that God was at work. God had used people in places far away, people that we met over fifteen years ago (like Michelle and

Lucy) to provide for us now, in the middle of this crisis that we couldn't have ever imagined nor foreseen.

Chapter Twelve - Every Day Adventures

The only thing normal about our new reality is that there is no normal. It felt like traveling back in time. Imagine traveling back in time, having the knowledge of technology and discoveries that are not yet created.

We have an electric gate, yet we must open it manually. We have a stove, a microwave, a toaster, a coffee maker, a blender and many other gadgets, yet we are cooking on a one burner gas grill. We have a fancy electronic washer that senses how much water to fill, yet we are hand washing our clothes every few days.

The island-wide system of wireless communication that once allowed you to pay for coffee in Adjuntas or an entrance ticket in El Yunque with your credit card is now down. If you need to buy something, you must first go to the bank and wait in line to withdraw money from your account and then go wait in line at the store to see if the product is even available.

It is like living in diminished reality, instead of the augmented reality that we were getting used to, thanks to technological advances. All of the sudden, everyday life became a series of adventures, hurdles to jump, and ways of discovering what we were really made of.

Some of us who are over 40 years old may have some memories of government food, from the now defunct program called PRERA. Back in the day, the federal government provided food to prevent hunger. I remember the black and white packages of powder milk, the block cheese, the canned pineapple juice, and the beans. After Maria, the food that the federal government brought was a combination of ready to eat military meals, called MREs, and non-perishable food from different sources.

People lined up for hours to get these one-person daily portions. Random items like Vienna sausages, granola bars and candy bars were paired with things like two small bottles of water and distributed freely wherever the government and the National Guard could set up a spot.

On more heroic efforts, military helicopters air lifted water and food to people stuck in mountain communities where the roads were impassible and seniors, children and sick people were seeing their food reserves disappear.

The scenes looked like they had been taken from a movie of a war torn country; including white-haired seniors meeting helicopters in fields, the wind from the blades blowing their clothes. There were old ladies with tears in their eyes hugging and thanking the young soldiers.

Update from the ark

November 1, 2017

42 days since Maria

Forty two days ago today, Puerto Rico experienced the strongest hurricane recorded since the 1920's. For close to twelve hours, most of the island was under winds gusts of 165+ mph. Thousands of families lost all of their earthly belongings. Many people died or were injured.

Since then, it is believed that over nine hundred people have died from causes directly or indirectly related to Hurricane Maria. This is not the official death toll, but rather a conclusion based on the increased number of deaths compared to the same period last year.

Our church has already attended a wake for the mother of one of our members, a lady in her 70s who suffered an asthma attack at night and died in her bed. Her asthma attack could have been triggered by the stress of not having essentials like water and electricity. Or maybe she needed to have respiratory therapy that night, but had no power to run her machine. Maybe the fumes from all the gas and diesel generators being used to power homes and businesses were too much for her lungs to take. We will never know; her family could not afford a burial, so authorities did not require an autopsy, and she was cremated.

On the other hand, while we say goodbye to some, others are being born who require much care to keep healthy. Mothers of newborns are concerned about pink eye and mosquito-related diseases. They are keeping a close watch on their little ones.

Nature is determined to survive. Leaves are sprouting on trees, hills are turning green again, and bees look for something sweet while they wait for new flowers to bloom. The water in many rivers and creeks has gone done to normal levels.

Some schools and businesses have reopened; many wonder how long they will manage to survive with increased expenses like gas/diesel and decreased clientele. Public schools struggle to reopen, given government bureaucracy.

According to the media, close to 60,000 people have left Puerto Rico and headed to the U.S. since Maria. Traffic is a mess; without power every intersection can become chaotic. Some intersections have US troopers directing traffic, some have street vendors, and yet others are like scenes from crazy foreign movies. We wonder if the 60,000 who left donated their cars to friends and family, because traffic has not decreased.

Grocery stores are recovering from losing all fresh food and the back log at the ports. Lines have declined and in many stores' lines have disappeared. Gas, batteries, and even bags of ice are more readily available.

On Sunday, members of our church donated nonperishable food items and hygiene products. Others donated cash. Yesterday, some ladies and I went shopping to supplement the donations, in order to prepare ten sets of groceries to give out to families in need.

As we approached the register, the cashier, a pretty lady in her late 50's, inquired if we were from an organization. Surprised, we said, "Yes, we are from a church." She mentioned that there were limits on certain items, but she was going to request permission from management to allow us to exceed those limits. Just weeks before, that now almost empty store had a line one hour long outside, and people were not allowed to purchase all the food they wanted.

The manager cleared us to purchase the food, which was probably a good business decision, considering the store was pretty empty and they were spending quite a bit of diesel to run it.

Those times of restricted shopping, lack of availability of products, and the long lines reminded me of a visit to Cuba some time ago. And to think that there such measures are normal, everyday life in that country, not too far from here. In Cuba, I remember stores with mainly empty shelves. People would wander in and ask, "What's for sale today?" to decide whether or not they would take the opportunity to purchase a common item (like an alarm clock) that they had not seen for sale in months.

Today, I got together with our pastor and some members of our church to pack the groceries, and then we went out in pairs to deliver them to people from the community. I learned a lot from the lady that I was paired with. Her name is Miriam. When we arrived at a home, she asked me to leave the goods in the car, and we just visited and talked with the folks. After about 10-15 minutes, she explained what we were doing on behalf of our church, and we handed them the bags, then prayed for them.

What a difference from the government-run places, where a couple of employees are behind a table, waiting for people to come, sign, and show ID, to then hand them a box with a couple of ready-to-eat military meals, a couple of bottles of water, and some candy bars. What if you lost your ID during the hurricane? What if you are too old or sickly to go claim your ration every other day? I just wondered how many folks are too depressed to even ask for help.

So, all of the experiences lived over the last forty some days had me thinking about Noah and the ark. If we were in the ark, instead of recovering from a hurricane, we would be on dry land by now. What would that mean in our context? Would we be back to work? Would we have electricity? Would we be celebrating that the worst is over?

I think of when Noah and his family got off the ark, and, after they built the altar for God and saw the rainbow, they had to adjust to their new reality. All their neighbors and friends were gone.

And what about the animals? Did they stay nearby or go back to the mountains and woods right away?

Noah and his family had been busy surviving for forty days and keeping the animals alive and perhaps praying for the rain to stop. And then what? How did they mourn the loss of the rest of all humanity? How did they recover? How did they move on? I would like to have that wisdom, right about now.

Maybe we need an additional forty days, but this time in the desert, like Jesus, praying and fasting for God to prepare us for the work ahead.

Staying strong in the ark,

Sandra

Chapter Thirteen - Let the Funerals Begin

With so many people dying, I knew that sooner or later we would be affected. Many of those that died were in poor health, and the aftermath of the hurricane was lethal for them.

In our culture, funerals are like big reunions, where you run into people you no longer see with any frequency: old friends, old neighbors, classmates, relatives, old church members, and people whom you lost touch with long time ago.

I've always thought that you should attend funerals to encourage the family members and help them feel less alone in their time of mourning. When my father died, this became so evident to me. I was touched by the company of many whom I was not expecting, like my hair dresser. I was also hurt by the absence of some friends and family members who didn't bother to show up or call.

Given this experience, I always make a point to attend funerals of friends' parents or people from the community, even if we were not that close. You don't have to say much; just show up and give them a hug.

Right after Hurricane Irma, we attended a funeral for the uncle of our friend, Juan José. His uncle was a relatively healthy man in his seventies. He was a retired drama teacher, actor, poet, and choir member. He had quite a voice and loved the performance arts.

During the hurricane, it had rained a lot, and water had accumulated in his garage. He went out to clear out the water and, while he was doing that, he had a massive and fatal heart attack.

When the family called 911, they were told that all services were suspended until the next day. So, his family had to keep his body on the floor of the garage over night with the door of the garage open to slow his deterioration. Can you imagine such pain? Having to sit and watch your husband or your father dead on the floor overnight!

After Maria, we read stories of people having to carry bodies into town because mud slides were blocking roads and nobody could go in to collect the cadavers.

Given the lack of electricity and the great number of deaths, funerals after the hurricane were extremely short. Some viewings were only four hours long, and then people were buried or cremated the same day.

The lack of communications and downed phone lines only complicated things for many who would find out about the death of a friend only after the burial had taken place.

And how do you comfort someone whose ninety-year-old father died in a car accident due to the lack of working street lights? Only God's peace that surpasses all understanding comforts us during these times of mourning on top of mourning.

Tuesday November 28, 2017

Sixty-nine days since the hurricane

Before the hurricane, our Church had started a Bible study series on the Fruit of the Spirit. After the hurricane, it feels like we have been in a particularly intense experiment on patience. It has not been easy to develop patience to its maximum capacity, but we hold steadfast.

We have had moments, long hours, and even entire days when it looks like we were going to fail the test, but, with the help of the Holy Spirit, we fight the good fight.

And I do not mean that we cannot feel indignation and disgust at our government's bureaucracy or even ineptitude. What I refer to is that, during these last two months, we have been tested in our Patience with capital "P." Everything is a trial, from long lines at the gasoline station and the bank to the insane traffic with

*non-working street lights everywhere. We have grown
and learned a lot. I hope we can remember these lessons.*

Chapter Fourteen - There Ain't No Such Thing as a Free Lunch

Having lived in Puerto Rico most of my life, I have grown accustomed to a world filled with laughter, creativity, and courage, but also resignation and a general sense of having been cheated.

Our political relationship to the United States of America has always been one of disadvantage. The U.S. has all the power to come in and apply their rules and regulations, while we resist, get cheated, and eventually move on to the next issue. We move on mainly because it is not a fair fight, but also because many generations, like mine, have grown used to the status quo. It's like experiencing a huge wave at sea on a row boat. Each Puertorrican sees their life as a small row boat, and, after crashing so many times into the waves, he or she turns around and lets the sea take the boat wherever it wants.

Less than eighteen months before Maria hit, another powerful storm had already swept through the island with great force. A body of fiscal overseers named by the U.S. President called "La Junta Fiscal" had its first meeting in Puerto Rico on September 2017 -- the result of the implementation of U.S. Law 5278, The Puerto Rico Oversight, Management, and Economic Stability Act (PROMESA). This law, signed by President Barack Obama in 2016, had the main purpose of restructuring Puerto Rico's debt to pay back over $100 billion to U.S. investors.

How can a tiny island accumulate such debt? The answer in short was greed. The municipal bonds issued by the Puerto Rico government meant that U.S. investors could earn tax free dividends. Who doesn't like tax free money? Unfortunately, too many irresponsible entities involved, such as investment bankers and Puerto Rico's government, were in charge of such "deals," and eventually the loans against the bonds were too great to be paid, and investors got caught in the middle.

Puerto Rico's economy is dependent on the U.S. almost entirely. I say "almost" because there is always criminal enterprises that can have money and drugs flowing in from other countries, but those don't pay taxes, so they don't count officially.

The U.S. keeps an old law on the books, The Foraker Act of 1900, requiring that all goods that enter or exit Puerto Rico do so in U.S. ships.

This increases the costs of all incoming products, and it also increases the costs of exporting Puerto Rico-made products. In a global economy, where things can be shipped from a factory in China to your doorstep, this law has crippled the possibilities of Puerto Rico's economy to grown.

If you add to this the years of neglecting local agriculture and other industries in favor of tax incentives to American manufacturing companies that were able to make huge profits here without having to invest locally or pay their fair share of taxes to sustain local infrastructure, then you get the perfect economic storm.

When Maria arrived on September 2017, Puerto Rico was broke. A board and a judge were deciding how to balance the budget. The Puerto Rico government had already tried to do this on their own, mainly by raiding the pensions of public employees, taking away worker's rights, and, my personal least favorite, giving huge incentives to foreign millionaires to come and set up shop in Puerto Rico. This last one was supposed to create jobs and bring an influx of cash to the local economy. The result: some millionaires are now richer by working the loopholes, and we still don't see all those new jobs or the positive impact that it was supposed to have on our economy.

Ironically, post-hurricane money is coming in. We are getting FEMA funds which will be used to fix homes and purchase cars, furniture, medication, and more. Also new federal funds were approved by Congress to support programs like Medicaid.

Companies that can afford it will be rebuilding their broken fences, blown up roofs, and damaged air conditioners.

Non-for-profit organizations are buying groceries and personal effects to distribute among the poor and those affected by the hurricane.

Those products purchased locally are an injection of cash. Some may be purchased directly from distributors, which cuts out the grocery store owners. There is a down side to disaster funds; they don't always improve the situation of the working class.

Take my friend, Lourdes, for example. Lourdes is a lawyer running a private firm in our city.

Before Maria, she was struggling. The once thriving industries of car and home sales generated enough clients for Lourdes to keep her business afloat, but, pre-Maria, both had declined significantly. The economic downturn hit her hard.

Now FEMA is offering "free" legal advice at their service centers. That means that, unless Lourdes has a friend get her a FEMA job, and unless she is willing to close her office and risk losing her current clients, there is no positive impact to her business. Quite the opposite: hurricane victims that could use free legal services will not knock on her door for help. Once FEMA leaves, those lawyers they hired for a few months will have to go back to their now empty offices and try to get new customers or recover the ones they neglected to go work for FEMA.

A similar issue affects other industries. While we are glad to see all the U.S. utility workers bringing electricity back to the island, they are paid more than local workers, and they will go back home in a few weeks and pay income taxes to their home states for work that was performed here.

The government of Puerto Rico announced that it will be selling stock for our Autoridad de Energía Eléctrica (AEE), which is the local agency that produces and sells electricity to the whole island.

Privatization of a bankrupt monopoly has very little chance of lowering the cost of energy to the island, at least not in the short term.

In the long term, AEE workers will experience a similar fate to the workers of the Puerto Rico Telephone Company when it was sold first to GTE and then to a Mexican company named Claro. Now we have lower rates, but service is terrible, and workers lost many union-negotiated benefits. The only consolation is that there are other phone companies that compete with Claro.

When the AEE goes private it, will be a monopoly, and only God knows how that will affect pricing and services. We can only hope that they do better than the company that administers the tolls on the expressway. They have contributed unfairly high fines, sneaky practices (no red lights to warn you at tolls), inconvenient systems, and hundreds of thousands in fines. The toll booth administration was not a deal for the people of Puerto Rico.

And what are we supposed to do? We can take the streets and protest, like the students and union did last year on May 1st. We can elect new senators, legislators, and mayors, like we have been doing in recent times, where even candidates running on independent platforms have won. We can refuse to pay our taxes, the tolls, and utility bills and live in the same conditions we lived in right after Maria. This last one is not a very attractive alternative.

> *Status Update*
> *81 days after the hurricane*
> *Dec 11, 2017*
>
> *Today, my nephew, Alvin, had a birthday. This was another reminder that life continues. The girls have been rehearsing special dances. They will be dancing angels in a Christmas Concert. Lydia's soccer team will play the semi-final game on Saturday. There is a lit*

Christmas tree in our living room, and school finals are approaching. It sounds normal, right?

Not quite. We still have no power, as do about half the residents of the island. For some people, this is very hard, as they cannot afford to gas up their generators on a daily basis. Others have older generators that stopped working. Residents of high rise buildings have energy for limited amounts of time, which also affects their access to running water.

Many small businesses went under, and others struggle to stay in the black. Most job openings are for store clerks and restaurant staffers, jobs left open by the thousands who left the country. Some public schools were closed for over two months, and some are still closed.

Community kitchens are still running, because hundreds of people depend on them for one hot meal a day.

Stress and depression are also rampant and cannot be ignored. The emotional toll of this tragedy is even reaching folks in other countries. Family members of Puertorricans have expressed that impotence and sadness are a heavy burden, while the distance makes it hard for them to feel like they are helping.

But we see hope every day in the efforts of hundreds of volunteers that take to the streets every weekend to help bring supplies and hope to families who are suffering the destruction of their homes and still face the financial impact of the hurricane that hit an already fragile economy. And in the hundreds of non-for-profit organizations, new and existing, that have reached way beyond their normal target audience. And we are so happy to see the church of Christ doing its job with care and compassion.

There are signs of hope everywhere. Today some electric poles arrived in our neighborhood. We were excited to see the workers and their trucks, because that means that we are that much closer to having electric power and getting rid of the horrible noise of the generators.

We keep learning what is really necessary, important, and cherished. Sometimes, in losing material things and comforts, we gain perspective.

Staying strong in Puerto Rico

Sandra

Chapter Fifteen - Christmas is Here

And it suddenly happened. We got our power back on Friday, December 15, 2017, around 11:30 p.m. The girls were already sleeping when we heard some fireworks, then a distant scream that sounded like someone was saying the power was back. I looked out the front window and the posts were still dark, it took a few minutes for the few street lights that still work to warm up. The most telling was the silence; people started turning off their generators.

That night, we slept with our mini battery fans on. Our electricity in the house was not connected to the street. Since we were running the whole house by connecting the electric box to the gasoline powered generator, we had to turn off the connection to the street to prevent power leaving our house and hurting workers who were repairing the lines.

The next morning, Michael got up early and figured out how to unhook the generator and connect us back to the grid. Thankfully, our refrigerator, stove, washer, and dryer had not been damaged, and they all worked. The overhead air conditioning (AC) unit in Lydia's room and the window unit in Irene's room seem to work fine. The AC in our room turned on, but the air didn't cool. That is the oldest of all the units, and it didn't resist the hurricane winds that pounded on it for the better part of eight hours.

Later that day, I discovered that there were about forty-two homes in our neighborhood that were still in the dark. When there is a cluster of homes that for some reason are not energized even though homes all around are back online, they call it a *bolsillo*, Spanish for pocket. It's both frustrating and maddening, because you know that the electric company will move on to energize other areas before they come back to take care of the problem in those pockets.

Irene was very happy that we could have electricity before Christmas. That is her favorite holiday. She loves to celebrate the birth of Christ, and both she and her sister Lydia enjoy our Christmas family traditions. It was Irene who insisted in putting up the Christmas tree; I wasn't too keen on it this year. Irene worked hard to place all the lights, even though we would only see them when the generator was turned on a few hours each night.

When the power came back, I was happy for Irene, but also for us. No more cooking outside or spending money on gasoline every couple of days. No more turning on and off the generator twice a day, and finally we could sleep with the ceiling fans on. What a relief from the annoying mosquitoes flying by my ears!

While I was happy for us, I could not entirely rejoice, as I knew many families had no electricity -- families with disabled children, bed-ridden seniors, and patients on oxygen or feeding machines. How unfair that we could celebrate with our lights on while many others were still in shelters or living with friends after losing their homes.

Christmas was actually a welcome celebration for many, because it provided a distraction from our tragedy and the opportunity to celebrate life with loved ones. It was like a celebration for survivors. Through social media, we saw how friends baked entire pigs and turkeys on open fires like the good old days. Nothing was going to prevent families from getting together to share a meal, sing carols, dance, or play games.

Churches carried on with Christmas services -- some in borrowed facilities, some without water or power. Nothing was keeping our Christmas spirit down. Even so, these were probably the most low-key Christmases in years. I suspect that the average household spent less than half their usual budget for presents and parties. Many employers limited their celebrations to a luncheon or postponed their parties until late January of 2018.

Chapter Sixteen - A Very Strange New Year

Since we moved back to Puerto Rico in the fall of 2009, our family has celebrated most New Year's Eves at my brother's house. My youngest brother Carlos is an extrovert with a bit of Type A personality mixed in.

Since we were children, Carlos loved sports and was not afraid of a challenge. Carlos and my oldest brother Alvin always managed to get fire crackers for New Year's Eve. The fireworks tradition remained even though Carlos is now a very safety conscious adult. Carlos was even a trained Fire Fighter for a local pharmaceutical company. So he would have us over to his house in Juncos to eat and celebrate the end of each year and the beginning of the next. Close to midnight, the kids will light up sparklers and play with noise makers while some of the adults will light up mini fireworks. The neighborhood sky will light up as many did the same thing all around the area.

But, as we said goodbye to one of the hardest years for our beloved country, my brother was thousands of miles away in Texas. He moved to the U.S. in the spring of 2016 to pursue a better job opportunity and try his luck. First he lived in Oregon, and then in 2017 he moved to Texas at the invitation of some former work colleagues who were working at a new pharmaceutical facility.

So we had no fireworks this year. Instead, we stayed home and invited my mother to spend the night with our family. I wasn't sure what to expect, but what we got was a 360-degree firework show. Our house overlooks the Turabo Valley. From our porch, we could see our neighborhood's fireworks display, the ones from downtown Caguas, plus the lights shooting up all around as far as the neighboring towns of Gurabo and San Lorenzo.

I guess, for most people, leaving 2017 behind was a relief. Anything coming ahead in 2018 had to be better than what we had gone through. For a few minutes between midnight and the New Year, we dared to dream of a better tomorrow.

The next day, on January 2nd, Michael and I celebrated our 19th wedding anniversary. We decided to continue a tradition we started two years ago and took a day trip to Old San Juan. This colonial city established by the Spaniards in the 1500s provides the perfect backdrop to a relaxing day traveling back in time through cobblestone streets and surrounded by charming buildings and imposing forts. And you see all of that while surrounded by the sea and the San Juan bay.

The hurricane had left Old San Juan almost untouched, except for knocking down power and hitting hard the people who live in La Perla, a poor neighborhood facing the ocean on the outside of the old city wall. At La Perla, many houses lost their roofs when Maria's strong winds hit the north of the island, while many feared that giant waves would engulf the neighborhood and swallow it whole.

I had never thought of how Old San Juan gets its electricity, but we learned that, in the old colonial city, electric posts were set up on the roofs of buildings. That makes sense, since the city was built before electricity was invented and there is no room in the crowded sidewalks to place electrical posts. That must have been quite the labor of love when it was first implemented, and now it meant that crews had to find ways to climb up most buildings and bring up cables, transformers, and wooden poles.

Old San Juan is a must-see for tourists who visit our island. On any given day, thousands of visitors come down from the big cruise ships to walk the streets of this old city and enjoy a day of history, leisure, and shopping. Thousands of people work inside the walls built to keep the city safe from invaders centuries ago. But Puertorrican families also love visiting, and they each have their favorite spots.

Over the years, we have developed a routine. We park in a public parking lot on the lower end of the city, near the piers. We then hop on the free trolley and go all the way up the narrow streets to one of the forts on the north coast of the island -- yes, Old San Juan is an island off the main island, but connected by bridges. Once we get there, we visit a fort, then walk our way back down, stop for lunch, and go window shopping all the way back to our car.

This time, it was different. The trolley was gone. It has not been operational since the storm. The parking was free, and there were definitely fewer locals in the city that day. The big cruise ships were all there, and thousands, mostly American, visitors were piling onto tour buses or taxis at the pier. We walked our way up to San Felipe del Morro, the main fort at the entry of the San Juan Bay. I found a spot in the shade while Michael and the girls set up kites to fly against the beautiful blue sky near the old cemetery. It was not as windy as they would have liked. It was hard to get the kites up in the air, but that didn't keep more than a dozen families with kids from trying. The area that leads to the fort is like a giant front yard with green grass to run around on and, more importantly, no wires or electric lines to block your kite.

It was nice to see all the tourists back. On the days following the hurricane, planes flying out were packed, but planes coming in only carried aid workers and supplies. It will probably take months for tourism to reach prior levels, and I wonder how long it will take for the industry to recover its financial losses.

On this visit, we had lunch at one of my favorite spots, a restaurant in the back of a souvenir store. It's an old inner court yard turned into a tiny restaurant. I can't ever remember the name of this place, but I like the fact that it's a hidden spot to eat and escape the crowds and the heat of the streets.

Chapter Seventeen - Maria Was Not the Only Storm of 2017

The year 2017 will be remembered as the year Hurricane Maria hit. Many will be forever marked by the disaster and chaos that they had to live through. They are thankful for having survived, but also scarred by its horror. This hurricane unveiled the reality that everything can change in a few hours and that safety based on financial wealth or possessions is nothing but an illusion.

For me, it was the second storm in one year. The first one, like a tornado, hit without much warning. On April 17, the Monday after Easter, I was fired from my job. Getting punched in the stomach would have been easier and less painful. Only a month before, I had received flying colors in my performance review, and even a bonus. Now I was being sent home for the first time in my life. Living in a country with high unemployment and having a rather unique skill set, losing a job can be scary. My faith in God sustained me, and, three days later, I was getting calls for job interviews. I figured everything was going to be OK. God had my back.

The days turned into weeks, the weeks into months, and no job prospects were panning out. Living on $133 of weekly unemployment check and our savings was scary. We tightened our belts and trusted the Lord to be our helper and our provider. His words once again kept me moving forward. While grocery shopping, I would hear Psalm 37:25, "I not seen the righteous forsaken, nor his seed begging for bread,"[4] resonating in my head.

As I meditated on the reasons I was given for having been dismissed, it made no sense. I was ashamed, sad, and mad, and feelings of betrayal visited me frequently.

Why didn't anyone stop this? How many people even tried to save my job? Anyone? And I wondered, "How can people strip others of the ability to feed their children, clothe them, and send them to

---

[4] Psalm 37:25 Holy Bible - King James Version

school based on dubious reasons? How could they sleep at night knowing that they had contributed to someone else's financial bankruptcy? All the while they act so carefully, because they knew they could be next.

And if that happened, how would they pay for their luxury cars or their expensive homes? How could they keep their summer apartments and their club memberships? How could they pay for their children's private schools and their home's mortgage?

After a few weeks, I decided that I was not going to stay in that state of self pity. After analyzing my actions and performance over the length of my tenure at that job, I came to the conclusion that I had nothing to be ashamed of, and I was not going to spend one more minute dwelling on it or plotting revenge. This was hard, especially since I had been treated unfairly and people had lied about me. Nevertheless, I decided to forgive and move forward. In the meantime, our bank account was moving only in one direction: down.

I had been thinking of starting my own company. I was not too thrilled about it, given that Michael is self-employed. Having two unstable incomes was not something that I ever wanted to do.

One day, after church, a member of our congregation, a man named Hector, approached me and found out I was looking for work. After a few more conversations, I ended up bringing him a freelance project proposal that he accepted. We met in his office on a Thursday afternoon. We discussed what he needed and what I could deliver. Hector and his wife kept the meeting short, since they needed to attend a funeral of a friend who had died unexpectedly.

A few days later, I found out that they had never made it to the funeral. Instead, they ended up in the hospital. Hector had a heart attack. So, here I was with my first client approving my first proposal, and now he was very sick in a hospital bed!

Needless to say, it was not a great outlook for my business. If it wasn't because Hector had already survived a stroke and had recovered one hundred percent from its side effects, I would have thought that the project was over, even before it started.

I knew that Hector was living on borrowed time, but I also knew that his project was an assignment from God. It was an idea that God had place in his mind over ten years prior to our first conversation. I decided to wait and trust in God.

Hector's recovery time became my training time. I researched and selected new software. I trained myself on how to make what I like to call the new generation of PowerPoint presentations -- videos. My project included learning how to edit sound and incorporate the narration. Before Hector was sent home from his month-long hospital stay, our first video was ready for its debut.

While I was working on my consulting business, I was also sending résumés and keeping my eyes on the job market. And then it happened again -- I got approached for a job, before the opening was even posted on the company's job board. I went to the first interview and passed.

The invitation to a second interview sounded a lot like a formality, given that the person knew me very well from working together on prior projects. After all, Puerto Rico is a small island, and the insurance industry is not that large. People change jobs, titles, and companies, but it's always the same crowd, more or less.

This is when my personal storm met hurricane season. The job interview was cancelled due to Hurricane Irma. Then it was rescheduled to the day before Hurricane Maria, so it got cancelled again.

A couple of weeks after Maria, when the company got their phone lines working again, I called. It took me a while to find the recruiter, given that her whole department was reassigned to a new area in the building. I finally got ahold of the recruiter, and, to my surprise, the job was still open. I was afraid that Maria would have made a dent in their recruitment budget. However, they never rescheduled my second interview. My friends in that company assured me that the job was still open, but the recruiter and the manager who had first invited me to apply stopped answering my calls and emails. It was another dead end.

Maria swept away a lot of small businesses. Many American stores took advantage of the devastation of their sites to close several stores in the island. This meant more unemployed people looking for jobs.

After things began to calm down, I went back to my job hunt. New opportunities seem to appear through FEMA and other aid organizations, but I was not getting called for jobs for which I knew I was qualified. And then it happened again -- through a former colleague, I got word of an opportunity. I knew I was overqualified, but I applied nevertheless. It took them like a month to call me for a phone interview, and that led to an in-person interview. I'm still waiting for them to make up their mind. Apparently, I'm still in the running, but a week turned into two and then into three, and hope is dwindling.

Chapter Eighteen - Each Day a New Challenge

Meanwhile, God kept opening doors for volunteer work. I had already been volunteering at my church since May, 2017, when we hired a pastor who was new to the area. I volunteered to accompany her on visits to the homes of church members, sick people in hospitals, and to funerals.

After Maria, I helped our facilities staff to submit the church's insurance claim. Our church lost the kitchen's roof, the only part of the building that was tin. We also suffered water damage, and the wind destroyed the water tank and some AC units. All in all, we sustained over $12,000 in damage, which, compared to other churches, was minor.

Insurance companies are so overwhelmed by claims that they are not abiding by the law that says that they must respond to a claim within ninety days. We are still waiting on insurance companies to respond to both the church's and our home's claims.

On social media, we saw the photos of churches that were leveled by the hurricane. One church lost all but a concrete half-bath. And pastors' homes were not exempt. There were two pastors whose homes' foundations were weakened by sliding terrain and another whose home got completely flooded, and she escaped by boat with her elderly mother when their whole neighborhood went under water.

In the midst of so much suffering and so little hope, I found that my days were better whenever I volunteered somewhere. The following post was from the day I went to a Salvation Army's storage facility to help pack food.

> *February 1, 2018*
>
> *It's been a little over four months since the hurricane, and there still so much to be done here in Puerto Rico.*

There are hundreds of thousands of homes with no electricity. And many homes still have no running water or only have service intermittently.

Many buildings remain in shambles, and there are remnants of the destruction everywhere.

Frustration and desperation are common feelings among residents and government officials.

In the midst of so much need, volunteers have arrived to help. Many are American utility workers and Christian volunteers. It is common to see these Americans having lunch or dinner at local restaurants or shopping for necessities at local stores.

This morning, a group of ladies from my old neighborhood and I volunteered at a local Salvation Army distribution center. We formed, labeled, and then filled up boxes with food. Each box contained rice, beans, canned ham, vegetables, soup, tuna, boxed milk, and apple sauce. There were enough essentials for perhaps a week's worth of dinners for a family of four.

We worked as fast as we could and filled up twelve pallets in half a day. On the other side of the warehouse, vans, trucks, and cars were being filled up with the boxes we had just created. The vehicles belong to churches, community organizations, soup kitchens, and similar institutions who are working in their neighborhood to fill the need for food.

For families still without power, the cost of gasoline for their generators places a big burden on their budgets. Many are not receiving any kind of government help. If they had insurance, most likely their claim was either denied or, like ours, has not even been processed.

FEMA has denied many requests for help, some due to technicalities.

The Salvation Army and the Red Cross are just two organizations feeding the hungry here these days. But there are many individuals, churches, and communities who have turned their frustration into action. Their work includes bringing food, cooking meals, helping with home repairs, purchasing furniture, and donating time and labor.

This morning went by real fast. We felt so good helping. We knew that those boxes will reach many homes in the next few days. Instead of sitting around feeling helpless, we placed our hands on the plow to prepare the land for the crop that is being planted in the hearts of many Puertorricans. Soon hope will grow.

Staying Strong,

Sandra

Chapter Nineteen - We Are Not the Same Anymore

We were living in a country with multiple realities. There were those who were employed, who had electricity and water, or whose homes suffered little or no damage. Then there were those whose homes were destroyed, whose jobs were lost, and who were not receiving answers from FEMA or their insurance companies.

On a given day, I would take a bag of groceries to someone in need, and, that same day, we would attend a birthday party. It was like traveling in time into an alternate reality.

While some Puertorricans were sleeping on the floor, fighting mosquitoes, others were shopping at the mall, going to the movies, or out to dinner. And the government was not doing much better. One day politicians were in Washington asking for more funds for hurricane victims, while the next day they were attending the opening of some ridiculous new business venture or announcing a new initiative that was really meant to pay back political favors.

It's hard to live in such contrasting realities. When you think about it, these parallel worlds have always co-existed -- we were just not aware of them in such close proximity. Our world is like a giant scale -- the more money the rich make, the poorer the people on the other side of the balance become.

God calls us to upset the worldly scales, to use our resources, our intelligence, and our power to bring justice, to feed the hungry, to clothe the naked, and to care for the orphans, the widows, and the aliens. We must say ENOUGH to the unjust laws that our governments keep passing. We must organize our own communities and establish our own agendas for the good of the people. We must come out of our hiding places and do the work God calls us to do, regardless of whether or not we think people deserve our help. And we must vote people into office who have servant hearts and not political ambitions of power and wealth.

Our dog, Sugar, seems to have developed canine post traumatic stress disorder.

At the first sign of rain, he gets very anxious and starts barking, something he only did before when it was thundering. We are definitely not the same anymore. Maria changed our lives forever. It has been a wake-up call for three plus million people. The real question is: what are we going to do about it? As for me, I know that I will Stay Strong!

Photo Gallery

Our home before Maria, ready with storm shutters in place.

As usual, we had our supply of candles and lanterns ready.

The sofa wedged between the door and the entertainment unit. Quick thinking saved our house from flooding.

Our side fence. One of many lost when Maria's fury tossed about all sorts of debris.

Our green porch right after the winds and the rain stopped. Our gas grill survived being tossed about against the walls.

Communications were greatly affected by Maria's winds. Telephone networks, Cable TV, and radio signals were all affected.

The puddle marks the spot where once stood our full grown lemon tree. It landed in our neighbors' back yard.

Trees were stripped of all their leaves, resembling winter in a cold-weather environment.

The golden arches of a McDonald's sign are now twisted metal

Maria's winds were so strong that they uprooted street signs, concrete and all.

Washing clothes by hand became part of the new normal. I found that the kitchen sink was the best spot for me to wash clothes.

Many homes depend on electricity for cooking. At public housing, gas stoves are prohibited. Imagine not being able to cook at home for three months!

We used disposable plates and cups to save the little water we had, but soon the stores ran out of paper plates and plastic cups.

We spent many hours on our green porch after Maria left us without power.

Irene, fourteen years old, sewing cushion covers to pass time.

Michael took advantage of the down time to catch up on his guitar playing.

A beautiful sunset in the midst of all the chaos. What a gift!

Irene reads the instructions on how to warm up an MRE.

When the stores finally reopened, some had no fresh produce for weeks. This was our local Wal-Mart.

Common scene sixty days after the hurricane. Malls and stores destroyed. Many were built following US standards; not ready for 125 mile-per-hour winds.

Eating out was like a reward to having survived being cooped up at home for many weeks. We hit the jackpot at this Denny's when we found the only electrical outlet in the whole place. It was time to charge our devices. We even brought our own multiplug (look by the ketchup bottle).

Unbelievable scenes of utility trucks arriving at our city to restore power.

Lydia, eleven years old, sitting on the roof of our home anticipating the power being restored. Our home was finally back on the grid on Dec 15, 2017, nearly three months after Maria.

We spent the morning of Saturday, December 23rd, at the Baptist Church of Yabucoa, bringing gifts to community children. The roof of the church took a hit; water was dripping inside. The whole town was without power. This was the town where Maria made landfall. There was devastation everywhere.

A world of parallel realities -- the malls celebrating the holidays while hundreds slept on the floor of their roofless homes.

This colorful scene is at La Perla in Old San Juan, January 2, 2018. Those blue tarps are covering people's homes.

Volunteers fill up boxes with groceries at the Salvation Army warehouse in Caguas. People are going hungry in Puerto Rico after the hurricane took away their jobs and the lack of electricity decimated their weekly budget.

Made in the USA
Lexington, KY
18 May 2018